"And One Was a Soldier"

Robert E. Lee

Mathew Brady, 1865

"And One Was a Soldier"

THE SPIRITUAL PILGRIMAGE OF ROBERT E. LEE

By

Bishop Robert R. Brown

WHITE MANE BOOKS

This White Mane Books publication
was printed by
Beidel Printing House, Inc.
63 West Burd Street
Shippensburg, PA 17257-0152 USA

In respect for the scholarship contained herein, the acid-free paper used in this book meets the guidelines for permanence and durability of the Committee on Production Guidelines for Book Longevity of the Council on Library Resources.

For a complete list of available publications
please write
White Mane Books
Division of White Mane Publishing Company, Inc.
P.O. Box 152
Shippensburg, PA 17257-0152 USA

Library of Congress Cataloging-in-Publication Data

Brown, Robert R. (Robert Raymond), 1910-1994.
    And one was a soldier : the spiritual pilgrimage of Robert E. Lee
/ by Robert R. Brown.
        p.   cm.
    Includes bibliographical references.
    ISBN 1-57249-118-3 (acid-free paper)
    1. Lee, Robert E. (Robert Edward), 1807-1870--Religion.
I. Title.
E467.1.L4B858   1998
973.73'092--dc21
    [b]   98-34566
                                                                    CIP

PRINTED IN THE UNITED STATES OF AMERICA

TO WARWICK

CONTENTS

PREFACE

This is neither a biography in the ordinary sense, nor an account of armies marching, trumpets sounding and battles raging. This is the story of the pilgrimage of Robert E. Lee toward a full-blown relationship with his God. Competent scholars have been studying the historic events of his life for over ten decades, but few have considered the inner spiritual forces which prompted them. As Thomas L. Connelly has said, they "have been content to describe Lee only in terms of his character traits, and have closed the book on his inner soul."[1] Consequently, what Lee was is well known, but little effort has been made to explain why. My task has been to examine that question.

In many ways, Lee was one of the most paradoxical men history has produced. Though a lover of peace, he was a professional soldier, and loyalty and duty first to his country and then to the state of Virginia plunged him into the death and destruction of war. An overall foe to slavery, at times he appeared to defend it. Seeking diligently after hope, he was often the victim of despair. In spite of these contradictions, he never lost control of himself or succumbed to events which would have destroyed ordinary men. He deepened his trust, expanded his beliefs in a loving God, and was never nearer to God than during moments of defeat and despondency. That has made him the prototype of what countless people would like to be.

To speak of his spirituality is to speak of the man himself, for his faith became the supporting timber of his life and his life the mirror of his faith. He is acclaimed for his gentle nature, his serenity and confidence in battle, and his strength in sorrow, but his virtues were not attained alone. God played a major role. God chose Lee before Lee chose God, and the depths of his faith derived from his willingness to accept and build upon the relationship God offered.

It is this relationship that I have tried to bring into focus. Lee's day is gone, and the culture he knew and loved is buried, but the example he left of possessing and being possessed by the Holy Spirit is always relevant—and contemporary. Let those who hate war and seek the advance of brotherhood examine the spiritual life of this good man. A poem written by Lesbia Scott in 1929, "I Sing A Song of the Saints of God," has become the lyrics of one of the Episcopal Church's most popular children's hymns. It names the various careers which non-Biblical saints have followed and in the process states, "And one was a soldier." Robert Lee was such a one and even a casual examination of his spiritual life will explain how with the help of God a person, any person, under any circumstances can fashion a friendship with God and in the process solidify character and create inner peace.

My approach to this subject has been topical rather than chronological, although I have used a chronological organization occasionally to show the progress of Lee's spiritual growth. Biblical quotations have been taken from the King James' Version which he knew so well, and when necessary I have indicated differences from the present edition of the Episcopal *Book of Common Prayer*. I have also left his punctuation, spelling and use of capital letters unchanged.

Of course, there is no way of measuring precisely the depth of his faith, particularly as he was such an uncommunicative man. This brings to mind the sensible statement of his esteemed biographer, Dr. Douglas Southall Freeman, that any attempt of a biographer to penetrate the mind of the person he is describing raises the danger of misinterpretation and distortion.[2] The risk may be even greater in respect to the soul. Nevertheless, I think the subject important enough to try.

In a few instances I have had to take what Lee said and did, make comparisons with the religious writings of less reticent autobiographies, and form my conclusions accordingly. Admittedly, some voids have still remained which defy measurement and have forced me to the level of educated conjectures.

One final point. An author, even on spiritual topics, is expected to be objective. That is well nigh impossible for me. If I were objective, I would probably not have begun this work in the first place. So let me confess my partisanship. I have been an ardent admirer of Robert E. Lee from my youth, and when I was rector of St. Paul's Episcopal Church in Richmond, Virginia, where he worshiped during the Civil War, I became even more conscious of the spiritual stature of the man. Then when I undertook a more definitive examination of his spiritual life, was surprised to find how easy it was to avoid pietism and sentimentality and let the facts speak for themselves.

ACKNOWLEDGMENTS

Considering its size, my gratitude for assistance in the preparation of this volume is extensive. The Most Reverend John E. Hines, former presiding bishop of the Episcopal Church, reviewed part of the manuscript and made valuable suggestions, as did the late Very Reverend Gray M. Blandy, the late dean of the Episcopal Theological Seminary of the Southwest. Thanks are also due to the late Clifford Dowdey, a good friend, who thought this work ought to be done, gave technical advice regarding it, and verified some lesser known facts of Lee's life and times. Gratitude is also due his co-worker, Dr. Louis Manarin of the Virginia State Library, for his review of the problems regarding Lee's oath of allegiance. Mr. John Jennings, Mr. Howson Cole and Mr. James Fleming of the Virginia Historical Society made research easy at Battle Abbey in Richmond. Mr. Jack Goodwin of the Bishop Payne Library at the Virginia Theological Seminary was equally kind in offering secular and religious books of the period, as was Miss Eleanor Brockenbrough of Richmond's Confederate Museum in making Lee's Prayer Book available to me. And a special thanks to Mr. and Mrs. Hill Carter of Shirley Plantation who spent valuable time sharing family anecdotes and some of Lee's post-war correspondence.

The Reverend William Sydnor, when rector of Christ Church, Alexandria, and the staff of St. Paul's Church, Richmond, graciously permitted examination of the records of these historic parishes. The late Canon George J. Cleaveland was particularly helpful in supplying volumes of sermons, biographies and autobiographies of the period from the library of the diocese of Virginia, along with his own monograph on "The Thirty-nine Articles." Dr. R. N. Latture, assistant in the president's office at Washington and Lee University, thoughtfully provided copies of an address and an article by two of his colleagues, Dr. David W. Sprunt and President Francis P. Gaines. The Right Reverend David Rose, when bishop of Southern Virginia, lent his personal copy of Marshall W. Fishwick's *Robert E. Lee: Churchman*. Mrs. Margaret Williams of Leesburg, Florida, and the Right Reverend Everett H. Jones of San Antonio, Texas, shared copies of family letters, and my sister-in-law, Mrs. Joseph L. Brown, lent books and articles on San Antonio history. My sincere appreciation to each of these helpful friends.

Others came to my aid loaning their family's copies of Confederate history. Captain Loren Fletcher Cole, U.S.A. (Retired) lent Fitzhugh Lee's personal volumes of J. E. Johnson's *Military Operations* and J. B. Hood's *Advance and Retreat*; Miss Nora Lee Antrim gave freely of her knowledge of the Lee and Fitzhugh families and arranged a pleasant afternoon at Shirley Plantation; Mrs. Edgar Carter Rust, Mrs. Hunter McGuire, Mrs. James Massey, Mr. MacDonald Wellford, Colonel Dabney Maury, U.S.A. (Retired), Mrs. James Bustard, Mrs. Howard Zachary, and Mr. John A. Conkle brought prized volumes from their libraries, several of which contained special bonuses of marginal notes written in longhand by former Confederate soldiers.

In particular, I am indebted to another sister-in-law, Mrs. Garrett Patteson of Fairfax, Virginia, for volumes from the library of her father, John Warwick Rust, some of which also contained written comments from family members who had served in the Army of Northern Virginia.

Each member of my immediate family was recruited. My daughter, Mrs. MacDonough Plant of Baltimore, provided researched items from that city. My other daughter, Mrs. Hollis Williams, Jr., Everett, Washington, found and supplied a number of references previously unknown to me. And my son, Justice Robert L. Brown of Little Rock, was especially helpful in researching items, providing notes on congressional action relating to Lee's restored citizenship, and serving for many hours as reader, editor, and critic. To each of them my love and special thanks.

As usual, I am chiefly indebted to my wife, Warwick, for her patient endurance during months of research and writing. Without her continued encouragement, innumerable trips to various libraries, and valuable suggestions, I doubt I would have begun this work, let alone completed it.

The family offers its deepest appreciation to Robert L. Brown. Without his extensive work, the publication of this book would not have been possible.

INTRODUCTION

A few years after the death of Bishop Robert Brown I had the privilege of staying in his lovely retreat, High Mitre, located on a mountain lake near Cashiers, North Carolina. In his venerable study, complete with his library and memorabilia, I wrote a good part of *Gump & Company*, the sequel to *Forrest Gump*. But one thing that struck me was that in the bookcases that lined the wall lay one of the better collections of Civil War literature I'd seen. Having recently completed my own Civil War history, *Shrouds of Glory*, I was both astonished and delighted to find this remarkable collection in so remote an area of the world. On solitary evenings I immersed myself in books I never knew existed.

Not long afterward I learned from Bishop Brown's son, Robert, that before he died the bishop had completed a Civil War history of his own, detailing the religious experiences of Robert E. Lee. This seemed to me an exciting revelation, for I was almost certain no one had attempted it before.

When Robert showed me a copy of *And One Was A Soldier* my expectations were more than fulfilled, for in addition to being a renowned cleric, Bishop Brown was also an accomplished historical scholar.

Few aside from true Civil War aficionados understand the importance of religion during that troubled epoch of American history. On the Southern side, especially, it carried a weight almost equal to the bullet, shot and shell. Lee himself was a devoutly spiritual man all his life and remained so through the most pitiless carnage this continent has ever seen. In *And One Was A Soldier*, Bishop Brown explores what might seem to be contradictions in a personality who on so many occasions personally sent thousands of men to slaughter or be slaughtered by their fellow Americans, and yet remained steadfast to his belief that a Divine inspiration was hovering behind the ghastly enterprise. So much Civil War historical ground has been well plowed by historians and others that it is truly refreshing to find a book on a subject that has barely been touched. While there are certainly fine general works on the influence of religion during the War, this is the only one I know of that explores the personal convictions of the most famous Civil War soldier of them all, General Robert E. Lee.

Winston Groom
High Hampton
Cashiers, N.C.
October 1997

CHRONOLOGY

January 19, 1807
: Born at Stratford Hall, Westmoreland County, Virginia.

1810–1811
: Moved to Alexandria, Virginia.

July 1, 1825
: Entered the United States Military Academy.

August 11, 1829
: Ordered to Cockespure Island, Georgia.

June 30, 1831
: Married Mary Anne Randolph Custis.

January, 1847
: Landed at Vera Cruz during war against Mexico.

September 1, 1852
: Appointed superintendent at West Point.

April 12, 1855
: Commanded Second Cavalry during Indian War in Texas.

October 21, 1857
: Obtained leave of absence to settle the estates of his deceased father-in-law, G. W. P. Custis.

October 17, 1859
: The insurrection at Harpers Ferry.

February 6, 1860
: Returned to Texas as temporary commander of the Military Department of Texas.

April 17, 1861
: Virginia passed the Ordinance of Secession. The news reached Alexandria on the nineteenth.

April 18, 1861
: Offered command of the Union forces.

April 23, 1861
> Accepted command of the military and naval forces of Virginia.

May 25, 1861
> Virginia military forces transferred to the Confederate States of America.

July 28, 1861
> Ordered to first field duty in western Virginia.

November 5, 1861
> Appointed to coastal defense work for Georgia, South Carolina and east Florida.

March 10, 1862
> Appointed military advisor to Confederate States President Jefferson Davis.

June 1, 1862
> Given command of eastern Virginia and North Carolina forces (Army of Northern Virginia), Seven Days' Battles.

1862–1865
> In succession led the Army of Northern Virginia in the Battles of Second Manassas, Sharpsburg, Fredericksburg, Chancellorsville, Gettysburg, Wilderness, Spotsylvania, Cold Harbor, and Petersburg (the defense of Richmond).

February 6, 1865
> Appointed commander in chief of all Confederate forces.

April 5, 1865
> Surrendered at Appomattox.

October 2, 1865
> Inducted as president of Washington College.

October 12, 1870
> Died at Lexington, Virginia.

PET FAMILY NAMES

"The Mim"
>His wife, Mary Anne Randolph Custis Lee.

"Daughter"
>His oldest daughter, Mary Custis Lee.

"Boo"
>Custis, his oldest son, George Washington Custis Lee.

"Annie"
>His second daughter, Annie Carter Lee.

"Rooney"
>His second son, William Henry Fitzhugh Lee, called Fitzhugh in later years.

"Precious Life"
>His youngest daughter, Mildred Childe Lee.

"Rob" — "Bertus"
>His youngest son, Robert E. Lee, Jr.

"Chass"
>Rooney's first wife, Charlotte Wickham.

"Tab"
>Rooney's second wife, Mary Tabb Bolling.

"Fitz"
>His nephew, another W. H. F. Lee, son of Sidney Smith Lee.

"Carter"
>His oldest brother, Charles Carter Lee.

"Ann Kinloch"
>Mrs. William L. Marshall, his oldest sister.

"Mildred"
>Mrs. E. V. Childe, his youngest sister, Catherine Mildred.

"Rose" — "Smith"
>Sidney Smith Lee, his brother.

"Harry"

His half brother, Henry, by his father's first wife. Sometimes called "Black Horse Harry," but never by the family.

"Markie"

Martha Custis Williams, one of his wife's young cousins.

CHAPTER ONE

A Climbing Instinct

The year 1807 fit quite comfortably into the first decade of the nineteenth century in young America. Although Europe was still in the shadow of its Napoleonic Age, the sun was shining brightly on the other side of the Atlantic. Thomas Jefferson was enjoying his second term as president, Seth Thomas was manufacturing clocks with interchangeable parts, and Robert Fulton's steamboat, *Claremont*, was working its way across the Hudson River from New York to New Jersey at five miles an hour. Average citizens were putting aside their memories of the war for independence in favor of agricultural and industrial growth. If anyone knew or cared that "Light Horse Harry Lee," the former cavalry hero, had fathered another son on January 19 it would have been a few veterans who lived in the area. This fact, however, was one of the most notable events of the year.

The infant Lee, named Robert Edward after his mother's two brothers, was born at Stratford Hall in Westmoreland County, Virginia. Stratford Hall was an imposing manor house built by Thomas Lee in 1732. It had housed a continuing succession of Lees, but not the Lees of Harry's branch of the family. Stratford came to him through his first wife, Matilda, a distant cousin, and she persuaded him to sign the manor house over by a deed of trust to their two sons, Philip and Henry, Jr. Philip died at the age of eight, making his younger brother the sole inheritor. When Henry, Jr. reached his majority, Harry relinquished his occupancy of Stratford Hall to him.

*****

Harry Lee had shown great daring and undoubted courage as a cavalryman. As a government official, he had served in the Virginia House of Delegates, in the Continental Congress, as governor of Virginia for three one-year terms, and as a member of the United States Congress where he offered the familiar tribute to his beloved George Washington, "First in war, first in peace and first in the hearts of his countrymen."[1] At one time, there was even serious talk of making him a possible successor to the first president. Yet the glory of those early years was all but extinguished by the shadow of the later ones.

The seeds of Harry Lee's destruction began with heavy speculation in plans to connect the Virginia-Maryland Great Falls area by canal with the mountain country of western Virginia. He purchased large tracts of land from the Fairfax estate for that purpose, but the canal was never built. Furthermore, the forty thousand dollars he lent to Robert Morris, a signer of the Declaration of Independence, for further land speculation was never repaid after Morris declared bankruptcy and was sentenced to jail. In addition, Harry proved an abysmal failure as a farmer. What overplanting did not destroy his crops, drought did. Unable to pay off his debts, he was sentenced twice to debtor's prison where he wrote his *Memoirs* in hopes that the sale would rescue him. But that, too, failed. Thus, atrocious judgment combined with bad luck to empty his purse, stain his reputation, and place him and his family in a precarious financial position from which it never recovered.

Harry Lee's wife and Robert's mother was Ann Hill Carter[2] of Shirley Plantation in Charles City County, Virginia. As the great-granddaughter of Robert "King" Carter and the daughter of one of the area's wealthiest men, Charles Carter, she was raised in style and ease. Her descent from comfortable security to the economic strain of Stratford required an application of many undiscovered virtues on her part. Her father's estate, large as it was, could provide only the barest necessities when divided among the twenty-one offspring of two marriages. In addition, an early invalidism had laid peaceful siege to her. Six children (the first died in infancy), long separations from her husband, and humiliating experiences with brusque and zealous debt collectors compounded her troubles.

Such dire circumstances might have transformed Ann into a cynic, but her love for her husband and children continued unspoiled and despite increasing illness promoted a cheerfulness which disguised the aches of heart and body. In time, pain forced the surrender of most of her domestic responsibilities, but she was always sustained by "the victory that overcometh the world . . . faith."[3]

Of course, the Harry Lees knew their finances would never permit a residence resembling Stratford, so when other prospects failed, they first had a modest home at 611 Commerce Street in Alexandria, Virginia, and finally at 607 Oranoco, also in Alexandria. Perhaps the selection of northern Virginia was due to Harry Lee's unwillingness to return to Richmond, where for so many years he had enjoyed public admiration and political power. Or possibly the many Lee and Fitzhugh relatives in the Alexandria area influenced the choice. At any rate, the decision was made, and the sad trek from Stratford began during the latter part of 1810.

The journey in rickety vehicles packed as they were with parents, children, and a few cherished possessions was an arduous one. The duty roads of the Northern Neck of Virginia were like corrugated washboards which could be reduced quickly by rain to quagmires. The tiny ferries which negotiated Virginia's swift streams were fragile and perilous. Be that as it may, no doubt the migration and adaptation to a new home in Alexandria were tremendously exciting for young Robert.

The years Robert spent in this small community by the Potomac River reflect little more than the boundless energy of a typical boy. In spite of demanding circumstances at home, there was enough time to satisfy his love of kite flying, ice skating, and chasing with other boys across the fields, after mounted fox hunters. It is even possible that he spied on the British fleet when it sailed up the river in August of 1814 toward Washington City, although more probably all the children were sent to relatives for safety.[4]

Of course, Robert had no understanding at the time of the financial misfortune which enveloped his family and certainly no foreshadowing of the calamities to come. Those who loved him were equally unknowing. Yet in their own ways, these adults became early influences on him through whom God conveyed the first hints of a protective faith.

*****

What Robert was to inherit from Ann and Harry Lee was of little monetary value, and this lack of financial prospects was to etch a frown on the face of his future father-in-law, George Washington Parke Custis of Arlington House. However, if his father and mother left him no financial legacy, they did leave an affinity and aptitude for moral and spiritual values which were to prove indispensable in his harsh days ahead.

Like many educated men of his day, Harry Lee was a deist who mixed a large helping of humanism with a belief in a personal but neutral and distant God. He also believed that by strict discipline and sturdy morality he could raise himself up to accomplish almost any task. This philosophy was a common offshoot of the Age of Enlightenment. The secrets of the universe which had been frozen in Dark Age superstitions were melted in the century before by the intellectual fires lit by men like Lord Bacon, Sir Isaac Newton, and John Locke — whose work was well known to college-bred Americans.

Harry Lee's correspondence with Carter, Robert's oldest brother, verified his allegiance to the intellectual movement. Marcus Aurelius was recommended for regular study, a piece of advice that Robert was to follow obediently, and John Locke, as political theorist, was suggested as the supreme authority on free inquiry and toleration. Alexander Pope, with his poetical essays on man, was preferred to John Milton and his fondness for angels. Strong emphasis was placed on the avoidance of debt, undoubtedly due to Harry's own weakness in this regard. There was little of the fatherhood of God and practically nothing of the divinity of Christ in his recommendations. Truthfulness and self-command were preached as the ultimate virtues.

Like many fathers of that era, Harry Lee readily confessed his dependence on Ann to train their children in the ways of character. In writing to Robert he expressed satisfaction that his ten year old would be confirmed in "his happy turn of mind by his ever-watchful and affectionate mother."[5] While most of Harry's correspondence was addressed to Carter and little to Robert or the other children, Robert clearly adored his father and absorbed much of his teachings on duty and honor.

But it was from his mother that Robert learned of God. The Carters had a tradition — instill into each child a loyalty, not only to family, but also to church and Creator. Family worship became a daily order, as was scripture reading. Sunday found the family pew fully occupied at nearby Westover Church, with the younger children often sitting out of sight on the floor. Those were duties every Carter owed the Creator, and Ann Lee was a Carter. As a consequence, she brought these principles into the Lee household, making family prayer a custom, instilling the basic elements of Christianity, and seeing that each young Lee attended Christ Church in Alexandria every Sunday. Her husband was amused, yet convinced, that in reality she was duplicating his own beliefs. As he said, she was "singularly pious from love of Almighty God and love of virtue" which, he insisted, were synonymous and not from fear of hell which he termed "a base, low influence."[6] Her kinsman, William H. Fitzhugh, called her "one of the finest women the State of Virginia has ever produced."[7]

Too little is known of Ann Carter Lee. A letter from her to Robert's brother, Sydney Smith Lee, while he was at sea urged him to resist temptation and to form strong moral and spiritual habits. Another letter written just prior to her death expressed a maternal concern for Robert's safety, while taking comfort in the faith that a merciful God would protect him. These are among the few firsthand glimpses that remain of her faith after the children were grown. But if you would know the mother, look at the son. The fact is that she taught Robert some never-to-be-forgotten lessons by cracking open the door to her soul so that, young as he was, he could see and never forget the awe, the mystery, and the love that resided there.

It was also from her that he learned duty and obligation — or rather as a result of her physical limitations. She had always been frail of body and the responsibility for growing children, the continuing concern for financial security, and the mounting anxiety over her husband's well-being, succeeded in overtaxing her physical resources by the time she was forty. As she ultimately gave in to what she called her "old troubles," this forced her youngest son, Robert, to assume most of the family chores.

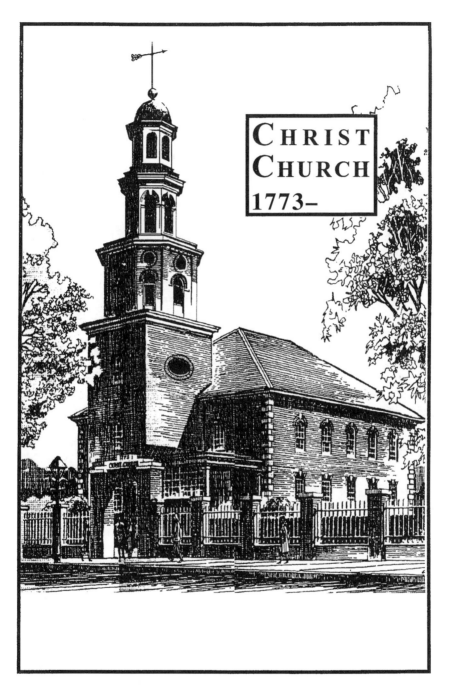

CHRIST
CHURCH
1773–

Robert E. Lee married Washington's step-great-granddaughter, Mary Custis, and attended Christ Church throughout his life when in the area. He was confirmed here, together with two of his daughters, by Assistant Bishop of Virginia John Johns on July 17, 1852. A silver plaque on the chancel rail marks the spot.

The Friends of Historic Christ Church

Robert had scarcely reached his teen years before he became the man of the house, and the problems of the Lee household continued unabated as his impetuous father manufactured further controversy. Harry Lee did not approve of his country's involvement in the War of 1812 and was quite vocal about it. He came to the aid of a Baltimore newspaper editor, Alexander Hanson, while on a visit to that city and along with his new found friend was viciously attacked by a drunken mob and left for dead. Perhaps it would have been more merciful had he died, for the shameful beating permanently disfigured his handsome face and crippled his once invincible spirit. In 1813, he fled to the island of Barbados in the West Indies to attempt a recovery among strangers, and it was from there that he penned his letters to his son, Carter. After five years, no longer able to endure separation from his family, he sailed for home. Becoming gravely ill en route he asked to be put ashore on Cumberland Island at Dungeness, Georgia, the home of his late friend and commander, General Nathaniel Greene. He died there and with the permission of Greene's daughter was buried in the family plot, bringing to a sad conclusion the life of one of America's most heroic yet tragic figures.

Harry's son, Carter, meanwhile, had entered Harvard University to study law and the second son, Smith, had received a midshipman's appointment from President James Monroe and gone to sea. Anne and Mildred, Robert's two sisters, were at home but one was a chronic invalid and the other an infant. It remained for their brother, Robert, to care for the horses, polish the carriage, serve as housekeeper, be the coachman for his mother's afternoon drives, minister to her as nurse and tend to Mildred as baby-sitter. When he later departed for the United States Military Academy at West Point in 1825, it is little wonder that Ann exclaimed, "How can I live without Robert? He is both a son and a daughter to me."[8] Yet, in the process she succeeded in indoctrinating him with worship habits and moral standards which formed the underpinnings of his indomitable faith.

*****

The first person other than his mother to exercise any spiritual influence on young Robert was the Reverend William Meade, who in time was to become the much beloved Episcopal bishop of Virginia.[9] When he arrived as the new rector of Christ Church in Alexandria, he was only twenty-one and still serving the required period as a deacon before his ordination to the priesthood. His stay at Christ Church was for a brief eighteen months, but he formed ties with the Lees during that short period which were never broken. Meade's affectionate manner together with his personal consecration and courageous leadership were much appreciated by the Lee household and were virtues that even a youngster like Robert could be made to understand and value. A typical example occurred shortly after his arrival when he learned that the vestrymen of the church had been holding festive suppers with a free flow of wine prior to their meetings. Young as he was, Meade rebuked the custom but with such tact that his abashed lay leaders never returned to it.

No record of Lee's baptism has ever been found. The habit in rural Virginia in the early nineteenth century was to bring the church to the child rather than the child to the church for the long horse and buggy drive between cradle and fort was considered too hazardous to an infant's health. Clergy, however, were notoriously careless about entering such house services in parish registers, and this undoubtedly was the case with the infant Lee. Even so, there can be no doubt of his baptism at either Stratford Hall or Shirley Plantation for in a letter his mother listed his deeply religious uncle, Dr. Robert Carter, as one of his godfathers.[10] Moreover, Robert could not have been confirmed later in the Episcopal Church had there been the least doubt of his baptism. Otherwise, a "conditional baptism" would have been required. Perhaps most telling of all, young Reverend Meade's well-known pastoral concern would have quickly uncovered such an omission, and he would have insisted upon remedying it.

While Robert learned his catechism at his mother's knee before he could read and write,[11] there was an additional requirement. Not only was a candidate expected to memorize the catechism prior to confirmation, fathers, mothers, masters, and mistresses were obligated to prepare their servants and apprentices as well as their children to recite it "openly in the Church." The *Book of Common Prayer* was quite specific about this. Its

Stratford Hall Plantation, Westmoreland Co., Virginia

Richard Cheek

instructive rubric respecting such public recitation used the obligatory "shall" rather than the permissive "may" and was taken quite seriously in early nineteenth century Virginia.[12]

There is no way to determine how frequently Meade heard Lee's recitations. Any influence he might have had on a four or five year old while living in Alexandria must have been minimal. Yet from his deathbed Meade remembered that he had heard Robert's recitations often. Certainly, Robert would have been too young then to have been tested openly in the church, so public or private examinations had to be made during Meade's later visits. Whatever the circumstances, the success of Lee's memory work was verified by the number of times he quoted from the catechism in instructive letters to his own children.

Although Sunday schools were not required and in fact were not instituted officially until the early twentieth century, it was customary for children to participate in church-related activities and learn by so doing. One activity young Robert was always eager to share in was decorating the church for Christmas. Also, his mother's wide range of religious interests and the nearness of the Lee home to the church down the street provided special opportunities for instructive discussions and social meetings when the rector came to call. Such occasions strengthened the boy's affection for his minister and caused him to feel at home in the congregation.

From childhood one of Lee's major inspirations and examples was George Washington. The noted Lee biographer, Dr. Douglas Southall Freeman, believed that he consciously imitated Washington both as boy and man.[13] There were Harry Lee's constant reminiscences about his "Beau Ideal" to support this influence. Also, there were the legends which were beginning to circulate around Alexandria about the nation's foremost soldier and first president, and later Mr. Custis's stories of Washington's family life. All of this fortified Lee's profound respect for Washington, and influenced his imitation of Washington's patience, courage, and discipline.

Among others whose personality and teachings molded young Robert was his maternal aunt, Elizabeth Carter Randolph. She operated a family school for Carter cousins of similar age at her home, Eastern View, in Fauquier County, Virginia. How long the boy attended is not known; nor is the number of his other visits. But he remembered his aunt as an affectionate person and a strict disciplinarian.

Another of Robert's teachers was William B. Leary who operated the Alexandria Academy. Robert was thirteen when he was enrolled there, and he remained in attendance for three years. Later, Leary supported his application for the military academy, acknowledging him to be well versed in the minor classics, Latin, and mathematics.[14] Prior to entering West Point, Lee also took a refresher course in mathematics under James Hallowell, a young Quaker, who had opened a school on Oranoco Street next door to the Lees. He called Lee "a most exemplary pupil in every respect."[15]

All three of these instructors had a marked influence on Robert, not only because of what they said, but because of who they were. His Aunt Elizabeth most probably conducted classes in religion; the others did not. But whether or not they taught Christianity, they lived it. At an early age, the fire of God's Holy Spirit began smoldering within Robert. In time. the inspiration and instruction of his parents, rector, Washington, teachers, and God Himself would cause the fire to burst into flame.

*****

One of the most influential guides in Robert's spiritual pilgrimage was his wife, Mary Anne Randolph Custis, the surviving child[16] of George Washington Parke Custis and Mary L. F. Custis and a goddaughter of Reverend Meade. The effect she had on her husband's spirituality is impossible to exaggerate. In later years, it would be her lot to remain in the shadow while Robert walked in the light of public acclaim for she also developed a crippling illness which prevented her from sharing in any but the most limited activity. Much like Robert's mother, she had profound and considerable spiritual depths, enhanced by a broad religious education.

In contrast to her husband's promptness and neatness, she had a notorious inability to keep appointments on time and her reputation for untidiness both in personal appearance and housekeeping became part of her lore. Neither was she as selfless and forgiving as her husband, and her outspoken scorn of Northern antagonists during the war, and of reconstruction leaders following it, was more familiar than her usual gentle nature. In pain and sorrow as in joy and celebration, the deeper side of Mary Lee showed a firm reliance upon God and a courageous acceptance of her fate. The warmth of her personality reached out affectionately to others on a one-to-one basis, moving those, who took time to know her, to become devoted friends.

Robert and Mary were romantic young lovers when they were married on June 30, 1831, in the dining room at Arlington Hall. The Reverend Reuel Keith, the principal of the nearby Virginia Theological Seminary, was at the time serving as rector of Christ Church in Alexandria as well. Lee was twenty-four and pictured as five feet, eleven inches tall with generous mouth, gentle dark brown eyes, and black wavy hair. As he stood before the minister, his sculptured features and graceful dignity aroused admiring whispers among the gathering.

If a portrait painted in Baltimore by William E. West several years later is any indication, Mary who was twenty-three at the time of her marriage, was possessed of a grave, full countenance, large deep-set eyes, a somewhat prominent nose, and a small mouth. She was not a classic beauty, but her gentility shown through. Robert was not the only young man whose eyes followed her with a flattering gaze.

At the ceremony, the Reverend Keith was less than prepossessing. A sudden rain storm had soaked him to the skin, forcing him to seek a change of clothing. The only wardrobe available, however, was that of Mr. Custis, who was short and stout while Dr. Keith was tall and lean. An astonishing picture resulted which fortunately was well hidden by the clergyman's vestments, but family members who had seen him without benefit of ecclesiastical camouflage could scarcely conceal their amusement.

The young couple's lives overflowed with sunshine and merriment in those early days. And from the beginning they consciously began to make preparation for the future by their mutual interest in things of the spirit. One of the qualities the groom admired in his bride was the viable faith upon which she fixed her course prior to the time that his own developed. In youthful, unselfconscious ways he discussed God and the nature of human existence with her. The library at Arlington, a large one for that day, was called upon to supply a variety of religious volumes which they explored together. As they talked and wrote about religious matters, sharing their thoughts and experiences, Robert found himself thinking seriously about Mary's God and the mysterious comfort and strength she derived from her faith. Others had provided facts and examples, but Mary brought God into focus and made the deity personal. She was not emotional about her religion, but God was real to her which had never been the case with Robert.

Robert grew in spirit, with Mary's devoted assistance. In the desperate days when war and fear and death struck with brute force, it was a pain-ridden Mary who sustained her husband with her unshakable belief in the inevitable triumph of goodness. Lee's correspondence exhibited how often he turned to her in anxiety over the health of his soul and his need for God's solace and guidance. If Robert's parents lighted the candle by which he could see God, and William Meade, George Washington, and his early teachers protected it against adverse winds, it was Mary Custis, who raised it high as a beacon to show him the way. Not enough recognition has been given to her many stellar, stalwart qualities, and knowing this, one of her daughters was outspoken in a wish that the world might know how worthy in every way her mother was of the man she married.

*****

Harry Lee's financial ineptitude and Ann Lee's chronic illness produced an initial shadow of adversity which hovered over their son. But with the aid of his mother and later his wife, Robert began to experience the promptings of faith which Dean W. P. Inge once described as a "climbing instinct, which draws us upward and onward."[17] True, it would remain for him to choose his own goals and the means of obtaining them, but he made a beginning with an intelligent appraisal of personal needs and a forthright appeal to Heaven for help. That approach, joined with the influence of others, opened the way to hope and the belief in unseen realities which the author of the Epistle to the Hebrews identified as "Faith."[18]

CHAPTER TWO

The Human Side

Like his eventual adversary, Abraham Lincoln, Robert E. Lee might well have said, "I have been driven many times upon my knees by the overwhelming conviction that I had no where else to go."[1] Both men had needs which human influence and inspiration could not meet. Both were drawn by their Lord's promise, "Come unto me all ye that labor and are heavy laden."[2] And both received strength and comfort from their God.

In the beginning others spurred Lee's interest in a spiritual life. But as he matured, he became aware of certain weaknesses within him which his mind identified but which only his will could correct. He could, of course, have resigned himself to these frailties, but instead he determined to correct them. He lifted up his hands to Heaven and in the words of the Woman of Canaan cried, "Lord, help me."[3] He had no where else to go.

*****

Surprisingly, homesickness was a weakness he perceived within himself. A military outpost was not the most congenial place in his day for a companionless man, and Lee suffered excruciating attacks of loneliness following graduation from West Point. Letters home were laden with longing because the intensity of his love for his family put him at such a low ebb whenever they were separated. Writing Mary from St. Louis in 1837, he complained that the separation cost him a pleasure for which there was no compensation. He was of the same mind ten years later when from Fort Hamilton on the Brooklyn side of New York harbor, he fretted over his solitude and complained that his only companions were his dog and his cat. Still later at Fort Brown on the Texas border in 1855, he grumbled that he was reduced to walking the banks of the Rio Grande River, picking wild flowers, watching animals as they scurried through the underbrush, and pinning his thoughts on his loved ones so many miles away.

Robert E. Lee did not know how to compensate for his separation from family. In spite of his obvious personal charm, there was a reserve about him which would not permit him to make friends easily. In his sixty-three years he could count his close friends on the fingers of one hand. While he participated, if somewhat reluctantly, in the social life the military base provided and threw himself eagerly into the engineering projects he was ordered to solve, his retiring nature could never quite overcome the timidity which controlled him in the presence of strangers or even casual acquaintances. If anything, social gatherings made him more acutely aware of his distance from home and family. A letter written from Louisville, Kentucky, in May of 1839 explained his condition precisely, "To be alone in a crowd is very solitary."[4]

Unexpectedly, his loneliness became a major factor in his spiritual development. When George Bernard Shaw's Joan of Arc was warned by the archbishop that unless she removed her armor and male habit he would excommunicate her and leave her alone, she replied, "Alone? I have always been alone. Do not seek to frighten me by telling me I am alone. I am alone and God is alone and what is my loneliness compared to the loneliness of God? God's loneliness is his strength. Well my loneliness will be my strength as well."[5]

The words are much too extravagant to apply to Lee, but their meaning is not. Instead of turning his back on spiritual values when separated from family and traditions, he returned to a custom that he and Mary had enjoyed at home—he took refuge in his books. In the process he renewed Bible reading and almost unconsciously transformed his drab bachelor quarters into a sanctuary of study and meditation. He found himself looking forward to these times of reverent solitude and eventually resented any intrusion upon them. Long before the Civil War, this study and discipline led to the discovery that while to be alone was one thing, to be alone with God was quite another.

*****

A second gnawing concern which drove Lee to his knees was a growing anxiety over the condition of his loved ones. Parental responsibility for the moral development and physical well-being of his children was a major preoccupation. So was his appointment as the executor of the estate of his father-in-law, G. W. P. Custis. But his greatest apprehension was over the status of Mary's health.

An infection following the birth of their second child was the beginning of a growing invalidism for Mary which evolved into rheumatoid arthritis. It swelled her feet and ankles and confined her to crutches or "a rolling chair." The birth of seven children in fourteen years did nothing to improve a condition which became more and more demanding. Mary lived with torturous pain most of her married life.

Lee's daughters were ready and able to assist with nursing duties, but when home, Lee preferred to assume the tasks himself. When duty took him away from these duties, he was careful to caution them about caring for their "poor mother," after he was dead. To the end, Mary's plight produced a vicarious suffering in him and constant frustration over her doubtful recovery.

His anxiety increased during the Civil War when Mary developed a total disregard for danger as she moved casually to visit friends, sometimes behind enemy lines, and at other times barely avoiding actual combat. Apparently, the possibility of retaliation against those who gave shelter to the wife of the Confederate commander never occurred to her. Neither did she consider that the enemy might decide to hold her as hostage, nor that there was an increasing number of marauding bands from both sides who were infesting the land.

Her indifference to these dangers was not prompted by illness or mental confusion, but by the gentle determination of a strong woman who simply refused to be hurried or ordered about. Her husband, try as he might, was unable to change her, and his pleas for caution and diplomacy were cast aside. He could only worry over her safety, her shelter, her supply of food and clothing. He wrote more desperate letters, and prayed "daily and almost hourly"[6] for her protection from attack and suffering.

Yet, like homesickness, anxiety over her condition resulted in a positive quest in his spiritual life. He could have lashed out resentfully against the added responsibility demanded by a chronic and willful invalid and convinced himself that her problems were only imaginary. Instead, he employed a substantial part of his prayer life to petition for Mary's cure and protection. Though she never received the restoration he prayed for, both Robert and Mary fell heir to a spiritual comfort and optimism they had never imagined possible. In itself this was a new experience. By praying selflessly night after night for his wife, Lee built the foundation for a more intimate relationship with God.

*****

The hazards of military life during the war with Mexico in 1847 presented a further dilemma. While his reaction to physical danger was assuredly not fraught with fear, it was more than haughty indifference. To say that he felt no alarm for his personal safety or relief when he passed through danger unharmed would be absurd. There was another reason for his anxiety—concern for the safety of others. A deep sadness over the dead and wounded of friend and foe alike were new experiences which became more and more of a spiritual encumbrance. Fear, compassion, and thanksgiving became intertwined as he cried out for more guidance and comfort.

Although Congress declared war against Mexico on May 13, 1846, for having invaded its territory and shed American blood north of the Rio Grande River,[7] it was not until August 17 of that year that Lee received orders to report to General John E. Wool for active service in Mexico. Five months later he was transferred to the headquarters of General Winfield Scott and landed with him at Vera Cruz. Lee's talent for reconnaissance became immediately evident in the battles at Cerro Gordo and the Pedregal, but the experiences also brought first-hand knowledge of the brutality of war and the suddenness of death.

On one occasion, an American sentry mistook Lee and his companion, Lieutenant P. G. T. Beauregard, for the enemy and fired, missing Lee so closely that the bullet singed his uniform. At Cerro Gordo, he was trapped at a spring and forced to lie beneath a log the entire day as the soldiers of General Santa Anna came for water. A wound he received while reconnoitering outside Chapultepec, though superficial, was a further reminder of life's uncertainty in battle.

General Scott was greatly impressed by Lee's ability and courage. After Cerro Gordo, he reported, "I am impelled to make special mention of the services of Captain R. E. Lee, engineer. This officer greatly distinguished himself in the siege of Vera Cruz, was again indefatigable during these operations, in reconnaissance as daring as laborious, and of utmost value. Nor was he less conspicuous in planting batteries and in conducting columns to check stations under the heavy fire of the enemy."[8] Later Scott wrote that Lee's scouting actions through the Pedregal were "the greatest feat of physical and moral courage performed by any individual in my knowledge pending the campaign."[9]

However, few men guessed what was occurring within Lee's soul during the war in Mexico. Outwardly, he displayed a quiet heroism, and only a rare release of pent-up emotion betrayed the inner tension which danger and death were creating. A case in point during the Mexican War involved his friend Joe Johnston (later General Johnston, C.S.A.). One day he arrived for a visit only moments after Johnston had received word of the death of his nephew. Unable to restrain his sympathy, Lee burst into tears. His concern for Johnston, for casualties on both sides, and for Mexican civilians also aroused his compassion and forced daily intercessions for God's intervention.

There came as a result of combat an astonishing revelation—he *was* being helped. An enthusiastic letter to Mary from Cerro Gordo reflects the profound impression that this fact had upon his faith. "I have endeavored to give thanks to our Heavenly Father for all his mercies to me, for his preservation of me through all the dangers I have passed, and all the blessings he has bestowed upon me for I know I fall short of my obligations."[10] There is nothing here of an empty Heaven or a neutral God. He was reacting as one who having witnessed death, was receiving the assurances of a personal, loving God and the benefits of a growing faith.

*****

Lee also suffered from bouts of depression. It is well to admit that the many attempts to canonize him have succeeded chiefly in dehumanizing him. If he had been all his worshippers claimed, his Olympian heights would have been too lofty ever to be scaled by mere mortals. He possessed no supernatural powers. Not even the mountain of fables which have grown up around him can overshadow the fact that he was a flesh and blood human being who was threatened by the same weaknesses which tempt us all. Moreover, being human, no degree of faith ever succeeded in controlling those frailties totally.

For instance, he was never able to withstand seizures of deep depression when everything that was right and good gave way in his mind to all that was wrong and evil. During his early military service, setbacks in his career, fancied or real, often tempted him to "bid an affectionate farewell to dear Uncle Sam."[11] Later when the years brought infuriatingly slow career advancement, he subjected himself to gloomy pronouncements regarding his failure as a soldier. Family affairs, particularly with his in-laws, could also upset him. He sounded like a spoiled child when he wrote his daughter Annie from Texas that it was probably best for him to stay away from Arlington, the Custis mansion, and those who resided there because his opinions differed so widely from theirs and besides he seemed to get in everyone's way.[12] And when secession seemed inevitable, he wrote despondently that he and his children would probably never see each other again.

Even after his military talents had been recognized and gained him a hero's reputation, these moods persisted. He hated defeat as much as anyone, and whenever his strategy went awry as commander of the Army of Northern Virginia, his reactions were extravagant. On one occasion, he complained mournfully that he was too old to counsel the army. On another he blamed failure on the fact that he could not get his orders obeyed. Then there was something far more desperate on that day when he studied the feeble state of his army just before Appomattox and was forced to conclude there was no alternative but to go to General Ulysses Grant and discuss terms of surrender. While he was reaching this bitter conclusion, reports were circulating (later proven false) about his sons — that his son Custis was dead, his son Rob was missing in action, and his son Rooney and his cousin Fitzhugh were surrounded and fighting for their lives in the adjacent woods.[13] Under this dark contingency, he pointed to the enemy's leveled guns close at hand and said to General Wade Hampton, "How easily I could get rid of all this and be at rest."[14]

Faith notwithstanding, the thought often tempted Lee that there was nothing to live for, work for, or pray for. To his credit, or because of the God he believed in, he waged a continuing war against his depression. With God he regained his trust and confidence following the hopelessness expressed in his statement to General Hampton at Appomattox. Having wished for death, he immediately paused, and almost physically executed a rightabout, and said quietly, "It is our duty to live." In his battles against gloom, the conviction that God had not forsaken him was his shield and the "duty to live" was his sword. He fought valiantly against despair with the end result being a restoration of comfort and peace.

*****

Colonel Charles S. Venable, one of Lee's aides, had no hesitancy in stating publicly that his commanding officer "had the high strung temper of a Washington."[15] This fact, muffled at times, in some instances has been justified anger against circumstances and events rather than people. At other times, it has been explained away as the consequence of momentary fatigue or illness. But there are too many instances which cannot be excused by such explanations. Those who knew him well were not exaggerating when they confessed that they sought to escape his presence whenever his face began to flush and his neck to twitch for they had learned from experience that the dam was about to break.

As a young officer he lashed out more than once against "the dirty — — —" in the nation's capitol whose slander he felt was destroying the reputation of his friend, John MacKay. Despite his ordinary respect for civil authority he could not control his wrath against the impotent Confederate Congress for its failure to supply his army, its occupation with trivial legislation, and its readiness to excuse social and political favorite sons from military service.

He seethed over the scorched-earth policy initiated by the Union army because of its inhumanity to noncombatants. The two Union generals he found most difficult to forgive were John Pope, one of the first to institute the policy, and Benjamin R. F. Butler, whose reckless orders reputedly threatened Southern women in New Orleans. Petty complaints and selfish grievances also struck sparks. Whenever possible Lee transferred grumbling visitors to a member of his staff. When one malcontent did succeed in reaching him, he reproached Colonel Venable afterwards saying, "Why did you permit that man to come to my tent and make me show my temper?"[16]

Lee is usually remembered for quiet dignity and patient self-control in knotty situations, but these virtues did not always prevent the sudden explosions of wrath. Another staff officer, Major Taylor was honest enough to admit that Lee was a man of "positive temperament and strong passions — and it is a mistake to suppose him otherwise."[17] Yet, at times his trust in God, his belief in the ultimate victory of righteousness, and his respect for his fellow man were simply not quite enough to curb the outbursts.

No one was more aware of this than Lee himself, more remorseful once his failure to control his feelings had occurred or more anxious to make amends thereafter. Once when his anger sparked a reaction from his aide, he said repentantly, "Major Taylor, when I lose my temper, don't let it make you angry."[18] On another occasion when he learned he had behaved unfairly to one of General J.E.B. Stuart's scouts, he ordered supper and hot coffee for the man, placed his own camp chair at his disposal, and spent valuable time playing host to the private soldier. When a young courier lost contact with his brigade while on a mission to General Ewell and presumed to approach him for directions, he was understandably annoyed. Bluntly he replied, "If you were where you belong you would know the location." When the boy-soldier explained the circumstances, Lee quickly said, "I beg your pardon," and sat down to draw a map showing the brigade's location.[19] Lee's wrath was real enough; just as real was the sincerity of his contrition.

*****

An inordinate pride in his ancestry at times was an annoyance for others. As a young officer, newly wed, he was not above bragging about his Lee and Carter bloodlines or his Custis wife's relationship to George Washington.[20] When he was thirty, he undertook an extensive two-year study of his genealogy, including a systematic search for a correct copy of the Lee coat of arms. Relatives and friends were enlisted to assist in the quest. There was satisfaction, too often expressed, in the discovery that his forbears had served as governors, part-time governors, in numerous legislative capacities, in judicial and military posts, and that two of them, Richard Henry Lee and Francis Lightfoot Lee, were members of the Continental Congress and signers of the Declaration of Independence. Richard Henry Lee was also the first to call for the dissolution of allegiance to the British Crown. It must have pleased him further to learn that he was descended from a line of gentleman soldiers dating back as far as the Crusades.

This belief in the importance of good bloodlines was reflected indirectly when he was stationed in Texas. On one occasion when riding with his young friend, John B. Hood (later general for C.S.A.), the conversation turned to matrimony. Fearing that in his loneliness Hood might choose hastily, Lee advised that a man should not marry unless into a family which would enable the children "to be proud of both sides of the house."[21]

His own familial pride might well have been nourished during his early career as a counterbalance to his supposed failure as a soldier. Though admiration rather than jealousy governed his attitude towards Mary's family, there may also have been an unconscious desire to show that the Lees belonged on the same social level as the Custises. His efforts to instill a knowledge of family in his children might have prompted the emphasis, or even his obvious love of history, but there was a defensive reason as well. Scandal at Stratford Hall occasioned by Lighthorse Harry Lee had aroused a burning desire to protect the family name.

No doubt his father's financial failures caused something of an embarrassment, but they were nothing compared to the moral failures of his half brother, Harry. The heir to Stratford, Harry, Jr., had grown into a shameful profligate and earned himself the title "*Black* Horse Harry" when it became known he was involved romantically with his wife's younger sister and, as custodian of her inheritance, had swindled her. He was forced to sell Stratford which had been in the family for so many years in order to make restitution for his embezzlement, and his stained reputation made it impossible for him to remain in Virginia. He set sail for Italy and eventually died a lonely exile in Paris. Lee, who in the early days had been extremely proud of his half brother, rarely mentioned him again. No son of his was named "Henry."

Whether all, or any, of the foregoing was sufficient cause for Lee's boundless pride in his family is subject to debate. It is worth adding nevertheless that even during the Civil War he was still reminding his grown sons of what a Lee should and should not do, and as late as 1869 he was elevating "The Family" in a thirty-four thousand word preface to his father's *Memoirs.*

*****

Despite the admiration of those who hailed him as the Southern Messiah, Lee's human deficiencies were not that heavily disguised. Loneliness and anxiety, fear and depression, anger and pride were readily apparent, and they presented a constant counterpoint to those who would idealize him. Even so, the singular fact about Lee is that he grew in faith and practice. These weaknesses, he confessed, were never totally corrected but they led him toward a growing certainty of God's solace and help. Though the threats to his character never diminished, his prayers opened an unexpected door to courage and hope. To paraphrase a line from Thornton Wilder, in Christ's service the wounded serve best.[22]

Lee's peers recognized this. Even his enemies suspected it. A single sentence from President Jefferson Davis's *Eulogy* to him is a fitting summary.

> This good citizen, this gallant soldier,
> this great general, this true patriot,
> has yet another praise —
> he was a true Christian.[23]

CHAPTER THREE

A Friendship with God

Dr. Marshall W. Fishwick has written that the only friend Lee had in all his life was God.[1] As exaggerated as the statement sounds, it cannot be discounted for one of the most conspicuous aspects of Lee's spirituality was the link which he forged between him and his Heavenly Father. A "friendship" indeed did grow out of the association because of an active God's disclosure and a searching man's absorption of what he *learned*. As the popular hymn reads:

> I sought the Lord, and afterward I knew
> He moved my soul to seek him seeking me.
> It was not I that found a savior true,
> No, I was found of thee.[2]

In keeping with his habitual reserve much of what Lee experienced alone in the relationship was kept to himself. Too little are recorded about the nights when he groped desperately for peace or the awe-filled moments when he stood in Christ's majestic light. When he shared his secrets with Mary, she was circumspect about disclosing them. That is unfortunate for judging from the results his personal experience with God could be of inestimable value to every seeker for redemption.

However, if there is little in the way of a first-hand account of his private spiritual encounters, there were a number of witnesses to relate his public ones. Family and friends had numerous opportunities to observe and analyze his worship. Clergy confidants were ready to express professional opinions, and not a few chosen attendants pinned their eyes on him at worship rather than on Heaven. They gave their impressions of him without reservation. Even today the maturing strength and courage he showed when tragic events and vital decision-making forced him to his knees can be discerned and judged. All of these witnesses confirm his "friendship" with God and verify the fact that there is no such thing as an unassisted, solely human, knowledge of God.

*****

Lee possessed an extraordinary sense of awe and reverence. Whether during the morning hours or late afternoon when occasion provided, he would mount Traveler and ride alone among the quiet hills to view the things of God, reflect, and drop the cares of life with a deep sigh. Whereas others might look down and see tangled undergrowth clinging to deepened tree trunks, he looked up and saw the beauties of nature in the dogwood's bloom, the cloud-rimmed mountains, and the sunset's glow. It was a time for listening and feeling. To the end of his days, he coveted these experiences when God spoke to him through the grandeur of nature.

Some theologians like St. Augustine distinguish God made known through natural religion from the God of historic religion — a distinction, if you will, between what God *is* and what God *does*. They agree, however, that the Christian revelation can only be expressed in active verbs.[3] Lee, of course, did not think in these terms, but he experienced God in nature and wrote of this constantly.

After riding through the Shenandoah Valley, he was moved to write Mary, "I enjoyed the mountains as I rode along. The views are magnificent — the valleys so beautiful, the scenery so peaceful. What a glorious world Almighty God has given us."[4] From Savannah, Georgia, he described the yellow jasmine, redbuds, and orange trees which perfumed the woods and the japonicas and azaleas covering the gardens. After reviewing the army at Brandy Station, he wrote, "What a beautiful world God in His loving kindness to His creatures, has given us."[5] After the war, riding to the Rockbridge baths he spied one of the most beautiful visions he had ever seen from the top of Jump Mountain and wrote his daughter-in-law, perhaps with a hint of depression, "My only pleasure is in my solitary evening rides which give me abundant opportunity for quiet thought."[6]

With such confessions there can be no doubt of the effect of God's revelation through natural religion upon this friendship.

*****

God's active revelation in historic religion had an even more pronounced impact on Lee. Three books provided most of the source material here. In the order of priority they were the *Holy Bible*, the Episcopal *Book of Common Prayer*, and the *Church Hymnal*. He preferred the Bible to any book ever written and accepted it as the infallible word of God. The fact that its teachings were inspired by the Holy Spirit was not debatable with him. Neither was the prayer book's injunction that "Holy Scripture containeth all things necessary to salvation."[7] As a consequence, he made it his textbook for daily living and the principal means for shaping his beliefs. Summing up its importance in a letter to Markie, a young cousin of Mary's, he said there was enough in it "to satisfy the most ardent thirst for knowledge; to open the way to true wisdom; and to teach the only road to salvation and eternal happiness."[8] For all these reasons, his approach was one of reverent reading in private and avid listening in public.

Lee's pocket edition of the Bible was a constant companion. It had been by his side from the time he was a lieutenant colonel in the United States Army and was on the bed stand almost as a talisman during his final illness. Its pages were finger stained from continual reading; its passages were underlined for emphasis, particularly those relating to salvation by grace and justification by faith. It would be next to impossible to single out other passages which were especially helpful. The Old Testament Book of Job which he quoted often; the Psalms, particularly the 23rd, 91st and 120th with their characteristic expressions of faith and hope for peace; the Epistle to the Romans on justification and the General Epistle of James on good works were certainly among the more useful.

Lee said once that Holy Scripture was "sufficient to satisfy all human desires."[9] When some English ladies sent him a copy of the Bible as a gift, in his letter of thanks he called it "a book in comparison with which all others in my eyes are of minor importance; and which in my perplexities and distresses has never failed to give me light and strength."[10] Quoting William Wilberforce, the nineteenth-century English philanthropist and abolitionist, he insisted, "read the Bible, so as to become acquainted with the experience and realities of religion."[11]

To a five year old who invited him to come to Sunday school, Lee admitted, "No one ever becomes too old to study the precious truths of the Bible.'[12] To his young namesake he advised, "above all things, learn at once to worship your Creator and to do His will as revealed in His Holy Book."[13]

During the Civil War he took time from military responsibilities to promote Bible distribution in order to extend "the inestimable knowledge of the priceless truths of the Bible."[14] After the war he accepted the presidency of a Bible society in a continued effort to spread God's word. Throughout his life Lee found comfort, security, inspiration and a never-ending hope in Holy Scripture. No wonder he gave it such an important place in his daily life. This was normal for one who found in it a roadmap for becoming a "friend of God."

*****

Next to the Bible, the *Book of Common Prayer* was Lee's most treasured possession. He had been fortunate as a child in that his family had a copy, for there was a scarcity of Church of England prayer books. During Colonial times and afterwards there were long delays in printing and shipping to the Episcopal Church in the United States. In the Lee and Carter homes, however, the prayer book, like the Bible was used diligently in private as well as public worship.

When his eyes became too weak to read the small print of the one he had from the time of the Mexican War, he exchanged it with Mrs. Churchill Gibson, wife of the rector of Grace Church in Petersburg, for several copies which he inscribed and gave to a chaplain for distribution.[15] The one he used during the remainder of his life, and his wife used after his death, had been given to him on Christmas Day of 1862 by Laura and Eunice Chilton, the daughters of General R. H. Chilton, who served as his chief of staff at the beginning of the war and had previously been with him in Texas. It was a prayer book-hymnal combination, printed in 1845 with large gold crosses impressed on the front and rear covers.

Then as now it contained a lectionary to aid in a systematic reading of the Bible. There were also Epistle and Gospel selections for Holy Communion each day of the week in the Christian calendar and the Psalms which he found so helpful arranged to be read in their entirety every thirty days. *The Articles of Religion* which were appended to it, the *Catechism* with its theological basis, and the Apostles and Nicene Creeds were also included. There were suitable prayers for private as well as public use. Among them were petitions *For Fair Weather,* an important factor in military as well as agricultural pursuits; a prayer *In Time of War and Tumult*, one *For Peace and Deliverance From Our Enemies*; and another *For a Sick Person.* No one can doubt their suitability to Lee's needs or their constant use. There were also, of course, offices for Daily Morning and Evening Prayers; and for The Holy Communion. Like Holy Scriptures, the prayer book served as his book of life by providing devotions for every important occasion in life from The Baptism of Infants to The Burial of the Dead.[16]

*****

For most people it would be unusual to accept a hymnal as a channel for divine revelation and friendship. Romanticism coupled with a Victorian sense of morality was at its height in the mid-nineteenth century. People reveled in their feelings and especially during the war were deeply moved by the pathos of such lines as Marie Reuenel De La Costoe's *Somebody's Darling;*[17] Elizabeth Bowers's *Dear Mother I've Come Home to Die;* and Benjamin Porter's *Ye Cavaliers of Dixie.* They made a practice of copying such lyrics on the fly leaves of their Bibles and prayer books, and when set to music sang them with tears streaming from their eyes.

Lee was as much of a Victorian sentimentalist as any of his peers and as susceptible to such emotion. He seems, however, to have been drawn to the words of the church's hymnal rather than to romantic music. While others were singing the words lustily during corporate worship, he was praying them.[18] There is no record of teasing comments by family members concerning an inability to carry a tune or any other evidence that he was tone deaf, so it must be assumed that his reserve in public was the reason he turned to the words rather than the music. Another was a concentration on what the hymn was *saying*. Like the Psalms, the hymns which spoke to his needs and promised God's initiative and help were the ones which captured his attention. Among them were "O For A Closer Walk With God" No. 683, "All Hail The Power Jesus' Name" No. 450, and "Rejoice, Rejoice, Believers" No. 68, but "How Firm A Foundation" No. 636 unquestionably headed the list.

When the congregation of St. Paul's Church in Richmond discovered Lee's favorite hymn, they made a habit of singing it whenever he was present. So, did other congregations on special occasions. It was also sung at his funeral in the Washington College Chapel in Lexington, Virginia. To read the words is to understand how they helped a man like Lee:

> How firm a foundation ye saints of the Lord,
> Is laid for your faith in his excellent word!
> What more can he say than to you he hath said,
> To you that for refuge to Jesus hath fled?
>
> Fear not, I am with thee, Oh be not dismayed!
> For I am thy God, and will still give thee aid;
> I'll strengthen thee, help thee, and cause thee to stand,
> Upheld by my righteous, omnipotent hand.
>
> When through the deep waters I call thee to go,
> The rivers of woe shall not thee overflow
> For I will be with thee, thy troubles to bless,
> And sanctify to thee, thy deepest distress.
>
> When through fiery trials thy pathway shall be,
> My grace all sufficient shall be thy supply;
> The flame shall not hurt thee, I only design
> Thy dross to consume, and thy gold to refine.
>
> The seed that to Jesus hath fled for repose,
> I will not, I will not desert to his foes;
> That soul, though all hell shall endeavor to shake,
> I'll never — no, never — no, never forsake.[19]

Many people are prone to overlook the promises in the words of sacred music, but it was not so with Lee. The faith and theology of this hymn and many others provided a much needed support during his "fiery trials." He read them as he read the Psalms, using their promises of God's love and all-sufficient Grace as the starting point for his prayers and meditations. Doubtless, that is the reason he preferred a prayer-book hymnal combination. Together they offered a practical avenue for his friendship with God.

There were other avenues through which God's inspiration came to him. For instance, he was a subscriber and ardent reader of *The Southern*

Churchman, an Episcopalian magazine published in Richmond and devoted more to instruction than to news. To illustrate, successive issues in 1861 carried articles concerning the theological reasoning behind *Conversion and Baptism, The Christian View of Death,* and *The Second Coming of Christ.* No one, least of all Lee, could read such articles and not be informed on the church's teachings. Moreover, even in the midst of war, or perhaps because of it, he was careful to keep his subscription paid and to arrange for its prompt delivery.

His friends among the clergy were another channel for God. These were Bishop William Meade, his first teacher at Christ Church, Alexandria; Bishop John Johns, bishop of Virginia; Dr. Packerd of the Virginia Theological Seminary; General W. U. Pendleton, an acclaimed clergyman as well as a graduate of the military academy at West Point; and Dr. Charles Minnigerode, the rector of St. Paul's Church in Richmond. Lee had opportunities to hear all of them from the pulpit and to read some of their published works. His affection for them and interest in their subjects made them regular contributors to his spiritual life.

Lee continually sought to reinforce his faith and convictions with other religious literature. On the day he was fatally stricken in 1870, he had a book which he may well have put down in order to attend the fatal vestry meeting at Grace Church in Lexington. It was *Our Children in Heaven* by William H. Holcombe and remains on the desk in his study at Washington and Lee University to this day. The book was a reminder of the tragic deaths of his daughter, Annie, his twin grandchildren, and his constant search for spiritual help.

It is doubtful that Lee could have given a chronological account of his passage into faith produced by all of the above. There was nothing in his conversion as dramatic as Paul's Damascus Road experience with its heavenly voice and blinding vision. Yet gradually his needs were leading to a greater receptivity to a God made manifest through nature and history as well as through his own devotions. It was as though having placed a pair of field glasses to his eyes, he was moved to adjust them until "someone" who had seemed far off and indistinct came into close, sharp focus.

There are many examples of faith and conversion. It is the trust Moses had when he crossed the Red Sea. It is what the Psalmist called putting one's "times" in the hands of God with reverence and total reliance.[20] It is the leper, the centurion, blind Bartimeus, and the woman of Canaan all reaching out with hope. And, of course, it is Paul writing to the Romans that the just shall live by faith.

C. S. Lewis, a layman and one of England's foremost authorities on Christian beliefs, had an undramatic conversion experience. Describing a visit to a London Zoo he wrote, "When I set out I did not believe that Jesus Christ is the Son of God, and when I reached the zoo I did. Yet I had not exactly spent the journey in thought. Nor in emotion."[21] It was as simple as that.

Understandably, Helen Keller's experience was far more personal. Deprived of eyes and ears and limited to faulty speech she said, "Down in the depths of my being I cried 'It is good to be alive!'. . . The world to which I awoke was still mysterious, but there was hope and love and God in it and nothing else mattered."[22]

Neither C. S. Lewis nor Helen Keller underwent cataclysmic conversions, but there was "hope and love and God" in their lives ever after. That was what Lee shared with them and with countless converted Christians down through the ages.

Admittedly, the precise date of Lee's conversion is hard to pinpoint. A few instances when he was a young husband and father suggest an early date for his new birth. Church activities at St. Louis and especially at Fort Hamilton show an increasing interest in the local parish. Gratitude for the birth of his children implies more than a casual acceptance of Providence. The most plausible explanation, however, is that God's gift of faith came between 1847 and 1848 during the war with Mexico. As important as his earlier responses were, they were milestones along the way. The battlefield brought a new consciousness of loneliness, a new concern over the sufferings and death of combatants, and a new awareness of personal damage. Military responsibilities had mounted and at home there was a new grief, this time over the death of his mother-in-law, Mrs. Custis. All of these experiences provided the climate for the blossoming of a full-grown faith. The certain fact is that during the Mexican War Lee began to write and speak with a pronounced conviction and warmth about a loving Father in Heaven who had guided and protected him and to whom he owed abundant gratitude. There was a greater certainty of a reachable deity, and a more vigorous confidence and courage seemed to emerge.

During this time a subtle yet perceptible softening of personality was evident to many outside his family. The strict moral character and manifest talent his peers had always admired were infused now with a greater glow of affectionate outreach which changed their respect for him to devotion. When he was ordered to Baltimore shortly after his return from Mexico, two ladies who had come to call on Mary were a bit awed to find the hero of Cerro Gordo at home and ready to enjoy their visit. He received them so graciously and put them at ease so deftly afterward one of them exclaimed, "Everybody and everything—his family, his friends, his horse, and his dog, loves Colonel Lee."[23]

In such ways the God-Lee relationship was producing the fruit of faith. The sometimes formidable "Marble Lee" of West Point days was being transformed into the revered commander of Confederate times, and to his military career was being added another career—a ministry to the poor in spirit. Now, having said "yes" to God's call, he was corroborating the words of Paul, "If any man be in Christ he is a new creature."

From the beginning, he confessed that the initiative for the relationship was God's. It was a conviction Mary and he had held in common most probably from the early days of their discussions at Arlington and Fort Monroe. When their daughter, Agnes, wrote from school at Staunton, Virginia, to tell of her spiritual awakening, Mary responded enthusiastically, but at the same time made very clear the primary role that God had played in the process. "God has sent His Spirit into your heart and drawn you to Himself," she wrote. "Remember what He says, 'Those who will seek me early shall find me.'"[24] Lee could identify with that.

*****

In the hundreds of biographies about Lee the watershed events of God's revelation and Lee's response are mentioned sparingly. The friend of God seems a far cry from the military strategist we see making his preparations to invade Maryland, or in that emotional moment determining to charge with his men in the Wilderness. It appears foreign also from the dignified aristocrat we watch making his graceful way from person to person at a social gathering. Yet that was the true Lee—the friend of God.

CHAPTER FOUR

Climbing the Altar Stairs

At the lowest ebb of the Second World War, Archbishop of Canterbury William Temple declared that "this world can be saved from political chaos and collapse by one thing only, and that is worship." Continuing, he added, "To worship is to quicken the conscience by the holiness of God, to feed the mind with the truth of God . . . to open the heart to the love of God, to devote his will to the purpose of God."[1] It is a definition that Lee met almost to the letter, for he possessed a conscience which could not rid itself of a source of unworthiness, a mind which searched unceasingly for greater spiritual knowledge, a heart which accepted the friendship of God, and a determination to obey the holy will of his Heavenly Father. All of these attributes called him to the type of prayer and worship defined by Archbishop Temple.

*****

There are as many kinds of prayer as there are words to make them, but generally they are reducible to a few major categories. Among them are adoration, peace, thanksgiving, penitence, oblation, intercession, and petition.[2] One of the most common is petition, illustrated by a bewildered Paul on the Damascus Road asking the risen Christ, whom he was en route to persecute, "Lord, what wilt thou have me to do?"[3]

Sometimes, the supplicant knows the answer full well but because of personal likes or dislikes rejects it. Often a strongly entrenched habit will lead the petitioner to choose an alternative. But the greatest struggle ensues when more than one moral principle is involved, and one is forced to choose between them. Then the pendulum of the mind swings back and forth from one side to the other, leaving one in an agony of indecision.

Lee's experience is a classic example. On February 4, 1861, he was ordered without explanation to leave Fort Mason, Texas, and report to General Winfield Scott in Washington. On arrival he was briefed by his aged commander in chief of the nation's plans for a new Union Army which was to be formed in response to the threat raised by the recently seceded Southern states. On April at the request of President Lincoln, Mr. Francis Blair, Sr. offered Lee command of this army of between 75,000 and 100,000 men. With deep regret Lee declined because he could not conceive leading a military force against the Southern states, in particular against Virginia, even though at this time it was thought that such an act would prevent war rather than instigate it. Returning to General Scott, he informed him of his decision. Scott, who was also a Virginian, disagreed and reluctantly told his protege that he had made the greatest mistake of his life and suggested that under the circumstances he might be wise to resign his commission in the United States Army.

At this point two contending principles collided within Lee — his loyalty to the Union and his love for his native state. Two months earlier he had shown his confusion when in a letter to Custis he said, "I am not pleased with the course of the 'Cotton States.'" He called them selfish, dictatorial, and threatening, and expressed his opposition to the slave trade "on every ground."[4] Yet, in a later letter to his father-in-law, G. W. P. Custis, he said, "The South, in my opinion, has been aggrieved by the acts of the North and are willing to take every proper step for redress." Then still again he reversed himself saying, "Secession is nothing but revolution," and back again, "Still, a Union that can only be maintained by swords and bayonets . . . has no charm for me."[5]

However, there was no escape, a choice had to be made. Virginia seceded from the Union on April 17, 1861, and the news was common knowledge in Alexandria by the nineteenth. Many times in the preceding months as the breach between North and South continued to widen, Lee insisted that he would never draw his sword save in defense of his native state.[6] Seemingly his mind was made up. But now that the literal choice was forced upon him, did he honestly mean what he said?

"Lord, what wilt thou have me to do?" He climbed the stairs at Arlington and closed the door to his room. He remained there until midnight. Mary listened as he paced back and forth overhead and thought that she heard him get down on his knees more than once. It was a precarious time. His father and his father's hero, George Washington, had risked everything in order to create the Union. Lee himself had given all of his own adult life to its preservation. The United States had educated him, trained him, supported him, and now was calling upon him in its hour of need. Moreover, if he should choose Virginia and the South, overnight a host of close friends could automatically become his enemies.

On the other hand, his roots were sunk deep in Virginia. It had been the home of the Lees since 1642. Stratford was there, his kinfolk were there, and in a very real sense the entire commonwealth was a "Rest and Relaxation" area for him after tours of duty in lonely outposts. It was also true that his father, in spite of considerable sacrifices to establish and maintain the young government, had continued to the end of his days to call Virginia his native land, answering without equivocation that in a crisis his first loyalty would be to her. That was his son's sentiment as well.

Understandably, the conflict between these contending loyalties, nation versus state, produced a quandary which he could not resolve alone. Personal feelings, public debates, and the convictions of others were not enough. Only Divine guidance could bring the pendulum of his mind to rest at one point or the other.

Since the maturing of Lee's faith, petitions for guidance were always motivated by the question, "What does God want me to do?" Whether the decision involved the resignation of his army commission, his involvement in a tragic, fratricidal war, or after four years of blood conflict his surrender of the Confederate army at Appomattox, the question was always the same. Its answer finally came that night at Arlington, and he sat down to write his resignation to the secretary of war. Two days later he accepted command of Virginia's military and naval forces and never called Arlington his home again.

To Lee's pleas for spiritual direction were added others of equal intensity — his petition for assistance. Like the woman who confronted Jesus on behalf of her afflicted daughter and cried out in desperation, "Lord, help me,"[7] he, too, being attacked by a multitude of afflictions throughout his life, called out to God.

The numbing shock of his daughter Annie's unexpected death in 1862 was almost more than he could manage. Surprisingly with three sons, two nephews, and a brother in uniform she proved to be the only war-time casualty in the Lee family. He had been aware of her illness at the White Sulpher Springs in North Carolina but was totally unprepared for her sudden death. When the message arrived, he was with his aide, Colonel Taylor, and Lee put it aside with masterful self-control in order to deal with the day's military correspondence, never hinting of the sorrow which was all but consuming him. Once the duty was done, however, and his aide departed, Lee took up the letter again. Knowing nothing of the tragedy, Taylor returned in a few minutes and without knocking entered to find his commander in chief sobbing, head in hands, with unrestrained grief.

Lee readily admitted that the anguish which accompanied Annie's death was pure agony, and the ache created by the thought that he would never see her again was unadulterated misery. Even months later he had found little relief for though the daylight hours were occupied with preparations for receiving General Ambrose Burnside's attack at Fredericksburg, there was nothing to lighten the load of his sorrow during the long dark nights. As he wrote his daughter, Mary, it was at those times that he was almost overwhelmed, for all his hopes seemed to be running out year after year, leaving him no alternative but to submit to his depression. It was the drain on his spiritual strength which made his prayer for help almost a daily call to heaven.

Faith nevertheless did support him, for often when he withdrew into what he believed to be an empty cell, he was surprised to find it occupied by God. If the throbbing pain of sorrow and despair tempted him to deny the validity of his prayers, it was nullified by a spiritual moisture which in the psalmist's words enable one to pass through the valley of misery and use it for a well.[8] When there are urgencies, there always seem to be ways to meet the accessible God. Lee climbed above his consuming grief over Annie's death and wrote Mary saying, "as in all things," a loving God had "mingled mercy with the blow by selecting the one best prepared to leave us."[9]

Whenever Lee turned to God for help he found, in addition to a clearer understanding of his faith, a readier compassion for others. In the process he also uncovered the surprising truth that by comforting others he himself was comforted. Thus, he was inspired to use the valley of misery as a well!

*****

In petition, one prays for personal needs; in intercession one pleads for the needs of others. It is well said that no one is truly related to another person until one prays for that person. The threefold intercession Jesus offered on behalf of his followers as he approached crucifixion is a classic example. Pleading for the maintenance of their faith, the continuing unity of their fellowship, and the protection of their lives against the world's hatred, he asked, "Keep them from the evil."[10]

It was a type of supplication Lee was taught to use as a small boy when praying for his absent father. We can be certain that he prayed in similar fashion for his mother as her infirmities increased. Marriage and the birth of his children became additional reasons for intercession. And as faith expanded vision, his prayer for the safety of family and friends extended to include all with whom he had contact or knowledge of a need.

Not surprisingly, he did not hesitate to seek the intercession of others. In the early days of the war, he asked old friends like the Reverend Cornelius to pray that God would grant him wisdom and strength necessary for his task. When the Reverend B. T. Lacy, the Presbyterian confidant of Stonewall Jackson, told him of the intercession being offered in his behalf, he broke into tears as he expressed his gratitude and confessed his need for all the prayers that could be offered for him. At Cold Harbor a chaplain who had rendered him a small service was surprised to receive an immediate acknowledgment and the statement, "I thank you especially that I have a place in your prayers."[11]

During an incident following the war, he expressed the wish that a certain long-praying Lexington parson would content himself by praying also for the Turks, the Chinese and other heathens at a different time.[12] Of course, accusations were soon levied that his rebuke of the parson's intercessions was too myopic. The remark, however, was only intended as dry humor, for a review of Lee's prayer life quickly showed how completely he believed in prayer for every sort and condition of person at home and abroad.

When Lee returned to Texas in 1855 following his superintendency at West Point (and his confirmation in the church), his "friendship" with God had deepened to the point where there was no self-consciousness in the prayers that he offered. A typical example is the understanding he had of God's initiative and love and his lack of hesitancy in sharing it with his wife during the lonely summer of 1855. "I must still pray to that glorious God without whom there is no help and with whom there is no danger. That He may guard and protect you all. . . ."[13]

His children were left in no doubt of his intercessions either. One exception to the non-religious character of most of his early correspondence was a letter penned to Mary during October of 1837 when though only thirty, with parental tenderness he confided, "I pray God to watch over and direct our efforts in guarding our dear little son."[14]

When Annie reached her sixteenth birthday, he sent congratulations from Savannah and confessed that he prayed night and day for God to protect and guide her. When his youngest son, Rob, was impatient to leave college and enlist in the Confederate army, Lee was not pleased, but he recognized the boy's right to decide for himself. So having offered a father's arguments, he stood aside and awaited his son's decision. That did not deter him, however, from praying earnestly for God to guide Rob to a correct conclusion.[15] At one point it seemed to him that another son, Rooney, was taking the need for divine protection too lightly, so he wrote his wife, Charlotte, proposing that she invite her husband to join them in regular supplication for God to cover him with the shadow of His almighty wings.[16]

It was the same with the other children. His open manner of speaking about God to them and the benediction with which he concluded his letters to them rang with a security and love which rarely failed to produce their grateful and affectionate response. Not only did the knowledge of his prayers increase their love for him, knowing his faith it gave them an almost superstitious confidence that the prayers would be answered because he was the intercessor.

All of Lee's intercessions were offered with a similar sincerity. As early as May 26, 1863, he expressed concern over Jefferson Davis's failing health and informed him that he was praying to a kind Providence to grant the Confederate president the strength necessary to meet the heavy demands of his office. When General Stonewall Jackson's condition worsened following the wounds received at Chancellorville, Lee's whole heart was in the message—"Tell him I am praying for him as I believe I have never prayed for myself."[17] His invitations in General Orders to military personnel to join with him and civilians throughout the South in prayers for the success of their cause carried the same authentic note. After Jefferson Davis was released from prison at Fort Monroe following the war, Lee told him his daily prayer "to the great Ruler of the World" had been that he would "be shielded from all evil and given peace which could not be taken away."[18] He prayed as conscientiously for the students at Washington College and particularly for their spiritual welfare. Then there were the intercessions for his enemies against whom, as he said, he had "never cherished bitter or vindictive feelings."[19]

It was fashionable in that Victorian time to tip one's hat to the deity. Concluding phrases of every day correspondence rarely failed to invoke the blessing of God. It was almost an unbreakable rule of courtesy and generally as meaningless as phrases like "yours truly" and "faithfully yours" are today. Yet Stonewall Jackson and Jefferson Davis reflected an unmistakable difference. So did General Lee. Conclusions in his correspondence were seldom stereotyped. Expressions like "may God guard you," "may God bless and preserve you," "may the great God of Heaven shower you with his blessings," carried his personality and gave off a benedictory note which could be taken literally and which still ring true in the twentieth century.

With the well-being of wife, children, friends, foes, soldiers, students, and government officials all weighing so heavily upon him, one would think he would have to make an intercessory list to remind him of the many for whom he prayed. But that was unnecessary. Their names were too deeply engraved on his heart to require any such aid to memory.

*****

Lee's childhood experience with family prayer was one of relaxed informality. Despite their precarious financial condition Ann and Lighthorse Harry Lee made scrupulous efforts to protect him and the other children from any hint of insecurity, and it is questionable whether the young Lees were ever aware of their parents' economic plight. Carter, their oldest son, recalled those times as happy ones when his mother played angel to him and the Fifth Commandment, "Honor thy father and thy mother" was given place next to deity itself. This was also true during Harry's absence when Ann was forced to assume her responsibilities as head of the house. The wholesome atmosphere of those early days strengthened the family's solidarity and made young Robert's introduction to prayer and worship a normal one with no suspicion of dread.

The same quality was to characterize Lee's own family prayers in the years to come. From the beginning of their marriage, he made a habit of reading to Mary each evening, then concluding with a chapter from the

Bible and a prayer from the prayer book. When in camp, circumstances occasionally dictated a change in this schedule, but there was never a substitute for it. His custom was to read the Bible and prayer book daily and, as he said, to draw comfort from their holy precepts. At home he followed the same routine but with a newly applied military precision.

After the war the mood of mellow simplicity was not unlike what he had known as a boy, but his children, grown now, never tired of joking behind his back about his lack of leniency regarding tardiness or absence. Even so their jokes could not hide their respect for the way he began each day with private devotions and when the family gathered, preferably before breakfast, this continued with readings from the Bible and prayer book. Apparently the use of extemporaneous prayers was rare.

When Rooney brought his new wife, "Tab," for a visit he warned her in advance that if she would please her father-in-law, she must be prompt for morning prayers. Lee was delighted with her punctuality and showed it, but Tab was to remark later with more than a grain of truth that she doubted George Washington himself would have been so ardently admired had he been late for the Lee's family worship. These congenial times when family members were drawn close through prayer were among the most gratifying moments of the day for Lee. Rarely did they fail to create an inner peace or to send him to his duties at Washington College with fresh anticipation.

*****

One of the most attractive features of his war-time worship was the unobtrusive way he had of joining others in corporate devotions. In March of 1862, having been ordered back to Richmond after unrewarding months in western Virginia and at the eastern coastal defenses, he found that the demands of the War Department gave scant opportunity for social engagements or even brief family visits. Even so, he made time each day to join a handful of worshippers for the 7:30 a.m. prayer service conducted by Dr. Charles Minnigerode at nearby St. Paul's Church in Richmond.

On more than one occasion he arrived unannounced and unescorted at General Jackson's headquarters for the dual purpose of attending worship services with him and meeting with his chaplains as a silent observer during their discussions and as an active participant during their prayers.

The incident at Mine Run in November 1863 is well known. When inspecting General A. P. Hill's lines one Sunday morning he came upon a group of private soldiers engaged in an impromptu prayer service. Without hesitation he dismounted, removed his hat, knelt and joined in the worship. His staff, of course, immediately followed suit. A similar incident occurred when the army was moving to the defense of Petersburg in 1864. Seeing a clergyman kneeling by the side of the road he halted and knelt with him to ask God for the necessary wisdom and strength in the coming campaign.

Such moments were of immeasurable value to Lee, not only because they provided opportunities for prayer, but also because they supplied the encouragement which came from a fellowship of Christian people sharing a common prayer with God. The almost pathetic manner in which he sought occasion for corporate worship reveals an unsuspected spiritual drought and a longing for an at-one-ness with other Christians. Numbers did not matter. Even when a pitiful few were present he seemed to receive comfort from the reminder, "When two or three are gathered together in my name, there am I in the midst of them."[20] Christ plus two were enough! A line from John Fawcett's familiar hymn further illustrates the point.

> Blest be the tie that binds
> our hearts in Jesus love;
>
> The fellowship of Christian minds
> is like to that above.[21]

*****

But as important as family prayer and corporate worship were to Lee, his greatest comfort, was derived from his private prayer life. These prayers seemed to offer him an experience in God's presence which went beyond anything he received in other ways. His rides alone into quiet natural surroundings and his custom of having his private service before family members joined him were important. However, the many special times when he stood before an open grave as the service was about to begin, or prepared to offer comfort to the wounded, or awaited the signal which opened a battle, cannot be overestimated.

In his way Lee wrestled as desperately with angels for a blessing as Jacob did, and, according to Mary, "sweated blood" in reaching conclusions which conformed to what he hoped God's plan for him was. Sleep came slowly at such times. There was a taut restlessness of mind, a laborious effort to bear the burden of harrowing sadness, and even, one suspects, a lingering hope that somehow the cup of responsibility might still be taken from him. So he continued his search and while what he found was not always what he wanted, it provided the spiritual infusion that he needed. Dwight Bradley described the feeling when he wrote:

> For worship
>   is a thirsty loud crying out for rain,
> It is a candle in the act of being kindled.
> It is a drop in quest of the ocean,
> It is a voice in the night calling for help,
> It is a soul standing in awe before the mystery
>   of the universe.
> It is time flowing into eternity,
>   . . . a man climbing the altar stairs to God.[22]

*****

One of Stonewall Jackson's servants was fond of saying he could always prophesy the military future by his general's prayers. Daily devotions did not disturb the servants, for they came in the routine order of things. But when Jackson rose in the middle of the night to pray, his servants would also rise to cook rations and to pack for they knew, "there will be hell to pay in the morning."[23]

Jackson prayed with fervor, Lee with quiet reverence. While there were times such as the midnight decision at Arlington, the refusal of command of the Union army and the grief suffered over Annie's death, when he wrestled with angels and sweated blood, in the main his prayers were offered with a serene faith.

By "climbing the altar stairs to God" he caught a spiritual glow which gave light to his character and direction to his conduct. Though his countenance had become creased with sadness in his last years, on occasion his devotions produced an enigmatic smile as though he was enjoying some enchanting secret with his Maker. No wonder a young Carter relative on finding him at Shirley Plantation one day and observing his general appearance, stared with awe and exclaimed, "We had heard of God but here was General Lee."[24]

CHAPTER FIVE

The Church—"I Will Give"

Over the years, Lee became devoted to the institutional church. After the war while living in Lexington, he became especially aware of the step-by-step, personal and corporate role it played in opening his life to God. However, long before that he began to absorb the attitudes his mother had exemplified. Rather than insisting upon Sunday worship as a stern obligation which often alienates a child, she led him to view worship as an opportunity to join others, both young and old, as they entered into the presence of God. This spiritual togetherness became an indispensable part of his devotional life.

Lee never equated the church with Heaven; nor did he genuflect before it as the infallible voice of God. He was too aware of its human limitations for that. But he did recognize a divine quality in its nature and a spirit in its ministry which overrode any temporal defects. His interest in local congregations sometimes resulted in a narrow parochialism; yet he possessed sufficient appreciation of the universal church as the guardian of Christian truth to keep him loyal to its international dimensions as well as to its local goals.

In time the church's ministry to his family and to him led to the realization of its worth. It baptized him, instructed him, solemnized his marriage, conducted the burial office for his loved ones, and ministered in numerous ways to his anxieties and griefs. Confirmation followed and with it official status as a communicant. He had cause to be grateful and loyal.

*****

He would have been much too young to remember the churches his parents attended during their residence at Stratford Hall. Nor could he have recalled worshipping at Westover Church near Shirley with his

36

Carter kinsmen when little more than an infant. Later he accompanied his mother on occasional visits to them and returned sentimentally more than once as a grown man. Christ Church in Alexandria, however, was his first spiritual home. Its tiered tower, capped by the cupola which was erected in his boyhood, and its white box pews, number 5 of which his hero, George Washington, occupied, symbolized the purity which to his young eyes was what a parish church ought to be.

He was forty-six when he was confirmed along with his daughters, Mary and Annie. The service was more private than public. It took place on Monday, July 17, 1853, at Christ Church with Bishop John Johns of Virginia officiating. Several theories have been advanced concerning the considerable delay of his confirmation. One was that Lee felt unworthy. Another which developed is that in those days children were not normally confirmed. His mother's illness could also have caused postponements. And Bishop Moore, Bishop William Meade's predecessor, might well have not been able to make a convenient visitation while serving as the rector of Monumental Church in Richmond. However, none of these arguments seem completely satisfactory.

The final decision to be confirmed, albeit a late one, is much easier to analyze. There was the example he wished to set for his children. Furthermore, as superintendent of the U.S. Military Academy at West Point, he believed he was in charge of the cadets' spiritual as well as their military education. Since his war experiences in Mexico, Christ had become so dominant a reality in his life that he could no longer delay in leveling the remaining barrier between himself and total allegiance. Christ's promise to be present whenever two or three are gathered together in His name had so deepened his conviction concerning the church as a "worshipping community," it now demanded a complete communicant status which only confirmation could provide.

Of course, confirmation was not "joining the Church." As the name implies, it was, and still is, a confirming of one's baptismal vows. In a sense, baptism is taking out one's citizenship in the church while confirmation is joining its army.

Lee never forgot the confirmation experience. The ceremonial "Laying on of Hands" as a form of lay ordination made it official. Now he possessed "the manifold gifts of Grace"[1] and an authentic place as a totally committed Christian. Bishop Johns made a lasting impression when at the conclusion of the confirmation service he said, "Colonel Lee, if you make a valiant soldier for Christ as you have made for your country, the Church will be as proud of you as your country now is."[2]

Like most Virginia Episcopalians, Lee was a "Low" churchman, that is, he belonged to a tradition which did not emphasize the ceremonial aspects of worship or its pageantry. The concern to avoid what were considered distasteful practices had existed from the earliest colonial days in that state and led many congregations to replace the altar with a holy table which remained unadorned without colored hangings, candles, or even a cross. Vested choirs were unknown. Clergymen wore no cassocks. A white surplice and stole were the customary vestment for celebrating Holy Communion, while a black gown together with preaching robe were usually worn for morning and evening prayer. Such a tradition appealed to the supplicant in Lee's nature, although he never found it difficult to feel at home with any form of worship whether it be the "High" Catholic tradition or the "Low" Protestant custom.

He and Mary made a habit of becoming involved in a church wherever his military duties took him — at Fort Monroe, St. Louis, Brooklyn, and Baltimore. Indeed, upon assignment to a new post finding a church home was one of the first acts of business. When alone in Mexico, he found an Episcopal chaplain and on occasion worshipped according to the *Book of Common Prayer*, but he also attended other services, including Roman Catholic masses celebrated in Spanish by native priests. In San Antonio he located tiny Trinity Mission. Later he worshipped in the temporary quarters of the new St. Mark's Church and contributed to its building fund.

*****

The paradox of Christian congregations praying for peace and supporting war is, of course, no novelty. History records numerous such contradictions where compromises were made according to what was considered to be the lesser of two evils. Christians have killed each other on myriad battlefields in the belief they were doing God a service. Not only did their churches minister to the suffering during such struggles, in almost every instance they adopted the cause of their governments with the assumption that they were helping establish the Kingdom of God on earth.[3] The preface of the *Book of Common Prayer*, signed in Philadelphia in October 1789, reads ". . . where in the course of Divine Providence these American states become independent with respect to civil government, their ecclesiastical independence was necessarily included."[4] Churches in the North and South were no exception.

So the die was cast when the Southern states voted one by one in favor of secession. On April 17, 1861, Virginia, the most populated and industrialized of them all, voted to leave the Union. Lee, who called himself "one of those dull creatures that cannot see the good of separation," prophesied "the beginning of sorrow."[5]

On October 16, the Episcopal Church in the South followed suit but on a high Christian level. Bishop Stephen Elliott of Georgia who was one of the conveners of the meeting adjourned it saying, "We shall be tempted to bitterness of feeling, to virulence of language, to impulsive actions, to conduct unbecoming the disciples of the meek and lowly Jesus." Then he added, "Let us strive while we render faithfully unto Caesar the things that are

Caesar's, to render likewise unto God the things that are God's."[6] No better words could have been chosen to represent Lee's point of view.

Still another convention was held in Augusta, Georgia, in November of 1862 to tie up loose ends with amendments to the constitution and canons and, on paper at least, the Episcopal Church of the Confederate States was established. A pastoral letter was issued by its bishops to be read in every congregation. In part, it said that slaves were not to be considered property but were a sacred trust which God wanted prepared to meet the work He planned for them.[7]

Bishop William Meade's sermon at the 1861 Convention of the Episcopal Diocese of Virginia echoed much of the thinking which governed ministers in every denomination. Lee, by then the military and naval commander of Virginia forces, took time from pressing duties to hear him. The bishop told how carefully he had avoided reference to political matters in the past, but that moral judgments had become so large a part of the issue, he now felt justified in making some comments. Stating his concern for law and order, and acknowledging all the blessings the United States had offered in the past, he explained how desperately he had clung to the hope that the Union might be preserved, but was forced to conclude that separation was necessary on religious grounds.[8] With touching solicitude he expressed a desire for church people and all citizens of the state to enter the conflict with "the most elevated Christian spirit, rising above all uncharitableness . . . and in addition to be "faithful soldiers of the cross as well as valiant and successful defenders of the state."[9]

The Southern clergy, following secession, did not find the transition easy. They were faced with the choice between the church which had baptized, confirmed, and ordained them, and a new rootless communion with an unknown factor. Some of them departed immediately for the North, others resigned their pulpits and enlisted as chaplains in the Confederate army, and those who were older were forced to gear themselves to whatever the rapidly moving events created.

The Episcopal Theological Seminary in Alexandria closed its doors in the spring of 1861. Thirty of the students were from the North and their leavetaking was a sorrowful one. The faculty at the seminary and the adjoining Episcopal High School were among the first to suffer for "traitorous activities" because they were among the first in occupied territory to refuse prayers for the president of the United States. Bishop Meade, Bishop Johns, and the Reverend Doctor J. F. McGuire of Episcopal High School were forced into the role of refugees.

Certainly, Mary Lee was not one to bow to the misfortune of war with passive resignation. Like legions of Southern women, she and her daughters knitted hundreds of pairs of socks for the army. She also joined in "Knitting Parties" to provide desperately needed clothing for service men, surgical tables for the hospitals and even removed cushions from church pews for pillows. At one point they were appointed to sew sand-bags for the fortification of Yorktown. They further established "Wayside Hospitals" throughout the South as short-time relief stations and provided food, clean bandages, and fresh clothing, all in their homes.

Despite all the pressures of military command Lee took time to con-duct a personal ministry of comfort and confession. Remembering the sick and wounded and the appalling treatment to which they were subjected, he gave away the food and clothing which was sent to him for personal use by well-wishers. With concern for the spiritual welfare of the men who carried bright and shining muskets but dressed in rags he also continued to search for capable pastors who could minister to them with understand-ing. To the best of his ability he kept abreast of major events in the lives of soldiers and civilians alike for he considered it his pastoral responsibility to weep with them in sorrow, laugh with them in joy, and by word and deed give them an example of faith-inspired fortitude. It was all a part of his Christian love.

Corporate worship comforted and sustained him during the war. Only the most pressing duties kept him from Sunday observances and then he was apt to complain, "One of the miseries of war is that there is no sab-bath."[10] His attitude continued to be one of reverent anticipation. True, he wrestled with angels sometimes in quest of guidance, but he was not a "Crisis Christian" who had to be faced with an emergency before attempt-ing to fortify weak hope with desperate prayer. Always he searched for God's will, praised His name, and gave thanks for His care while taking peace and solace in His presence.

From the moment Lee arrived in Richmond and took up residence at the Spottswood Hotel in 1861, he began to worship at St. Paul's Church at Ninth and Grace Streets. Later in 1862, Mary Lee leased a home on Leigh Street between Second and Third. The Lees faithfully attended St. Paul's and occupied a pew on the west side of the church which is marked to this day by a bronze plaque. President Jefferson Davis also attended St. Paul's. If Mary Lee's crippled condition prevented her attendance at church, she followed the service with her prayer book at home, but her daughters were always present at St. Paul's as were her sons and husband when they could take time from military duties. The congregation rarely failed to mark Lee's presence by some unspoken expression of gratitude and admiration as much for his Christian example as for his military leadership. On his return from Gettysburg, the members remained in their pews at the conclusion of the service and offered a silent, standing tribute as he walked slowly up the aisle.

The slight difference between the "new" Southern churches and the old Northern ones in no way affected the spiritual fellowship Lee so des-perately needed. He continued to value them both as parts of the church of God for despite battle and blood and death at least three basic qualities had not changed. First, the self-sacrificing efforts of the members to relieve suffering and ease pain; secondly, the unity created and expressed in their worshipping community; and thirdly, the guidance of God he found there which became for him a pillar of cloud by day and a pillar of fire by night.

*****

To the surprise of everyone, following Appomattox Lee accepted his election as president of Washington College in Lexington, Virginia, and proceeded with the monumental task of raising endowments, repairing buildings, and updating and staff. There was a strong spiritual compulsion behind his decision, but even so, it is doubtful that the trauma of adjustments he was forced to make can be overestimated. The transition from war to peace, from soldier to educator, and from plantation life in northeastern Virginia to the more rustic tastes of the Shenandoah Valley were equally difficult.

There were other negative aspects. The countryside had been thoroughly despoiled by the North's scorched-earth policy. A small but influential number of United States congressmen seemed determined to reverse President Lincoln's plea for amnesty and extract their pound of flesh from the South in general and from its leaders in particular. In addition, Lee was well aware of his failing health and made no secret of the fact that at best he had only a few years to live.

His first act at Washington College, even before the construction of adequate living quarters for himself and family, and before the establishment of office space, was to make plans for a new chapel on the campus. Perhaps he was thinking back to his West Point days when as a cadet he was forced to attend services in unattractive surroundings. Certainly, he was building on the conviction that a young man's preparation for life should include a proper grounding in Christian faith and practice. A sound mind and a sound body were like two legs of a three-legged stool. Without the third, a sound spirit, it could support nothing.

The chapel notwithstanding, the only normal parish congregation Lee can be said to have enjoyed since entering the U.S. Military Academy in 1824 was Grace Church in Lexington. Like every other institution in the area, its treasury was depleted, its building in desperate need of repair and its congregation impoverished. But it was still "the Body of Christ" and as such had as much claim to his loyalty as the college chapel. The task of rebuilding was daunting. With a touch of humor he admitted to daughter Mildred that Episcopalians in the community were "few in number and light in purse."[11]

Scarcely had he dismounted from Traveler at the Lexington Hotel before he was elected on September 26, 1865, to the vestry of the church. He took his election seriously and served willingly both as chairman of the Vestry's Committee on Finance and as a member of its Building Committee.

Lee Chapel at Washington and Lee University

W. Patrick Hinely, Washington and Lee University

In these connections two facts were self-evident and he made no effort to sidestep them. First, $800 a year was an "insufficient salary for the decent support of the Pastor."[12] Moreover, he was convinced, "Resolutions will not build the church. It will require money."[13] Accordingly, he set out to raise funds for both projects.

The Grace Church congregation was extremely proud of its illustrious communicant and anxious to show him off at as many parochial and nonparochial events as possible. It was a foregone conclusion that he would be elected as a delegate to the annual Council of the Diocese of Virginia which met first at St. Paul's Church in Lynchburg and then at St. George's Church in Fredericksburg. At both councils, he was appointed to the Committee on the State of the Church as well as to the Committee on Clergy Salaries. At Lynchburg he was also nominated as a deputy to the General Convention of the National Church but tactfully refused, probably to avoid having his name associated with any national enterprise which could prove to be an embarrassment.

In addition, he was elected president of the Rockbridge Bible Society and espoused the cause of the College Young Men's Christian Association. Campus revivals also received his hearty support, and regardless of denomination, visiting ministers to the campus were extended invitations to preach at the chapel while local ministers were asked to serve as chaplains to the students who were members of their denominations. It was well said of Lee that he was devoted to Christianity, not "churchianity," and while his loyalty to the Episcopal Church remained constant, he fervently believed that every individual should be free to affiliate with whatever creed and engage in whatever form of worship which could bring that person closer to God.

It is not surprising, but it is eminently fitting, that Lee's final public appearance was to be at his church. A vestry meeting had been called at Grace Church to consider its two major problems: the building program and the rector's stipend. Lee should have remained at home on that bleak, rainy September day in 1870 and treated his deep chest cold but as on so many other occasions, his sense of duty outweighed his common sense. Prophetically, his daughter, Mildred, was at the piano playing Mendelssohn's "Funeral March" as he departed. Making his way to the dank, unheated church, he chaired the meeting for three hours with his usual great dignity.

Reverend Pendleton's stipend had always been inadequate and usually in arrears. It was the unanimous desire to remedy that injustice and each member made an additional pledge according to his means. Still, the sum was $55.00 short of the desired amount. Quietly, Lee said, "I will give that sum."[14]

It was seven o'clock before he could make his way back up the hill to his home in the gathering night. Dinner was waiting and Mary expressed some impatience as he joined the family already at the table. He smiled, but when he attempted to say the customary grace he suddenly collapsed in his chair, conscious but unable to speak. The bankruptcy of his physical resources had finally come.

He did not seem to want to recover from what Drs. R. L. Madison and Howard T. Barton diagnosed as "Venous congestion of the brain" (cerebral thrombosis).[15] Finally, on October 12, 1870, at 9:30 in the morning, Lee gave his last command. "Strike the tent,"[16] he whispered. A few hours later, with Mary and Rev. Pendleton at his side, he entered into a "life of perfect service" in God's "Heavenly Kingdom."

After his death the members of the Grace Church congregation chose another name for their parish: "The Robert E. Lee Memorial Church." In time Washington College added his name, becoming Washington and Lee University. With some justification admirers in every age might recall the words of St. Paul, "I have fought the good fight, I have finished my course, I have kept the faith."[17] However, Lee's last public words at his last public meeting can serve as an even more appropriate epitaph of his God-centered life and works: "I will give."

CHAPTER SIX

"I Believe"

The essential goal of religious faith is to build a relationship with the eternal God premised on trust and devotion. The essential goal of theology is to understand God in time. It is well said then, in light of these precepts, that while faith is centered in Heaven, theology is centered on earth. Because it is earth-bound, theology, as Dr. Gordon D. Kaufman has written, is "a human approach, subject to contemporary conditions, concerned with God's revelations, and more basic still with questions about him." In other words, "Theology interprets what it discovers in faith."[1]

It is doubtful that Lee was ever concerned about this distinction. Not for a moment did he deny the necessity of a rational faith, but he "felt" his spiritual experiences so strongly that he was never quite willing to reduce it to somber words. Even so, though unconsciously, he possessed a surprisingly orthodox theology.

His beliefs were never carelessly adopted. What he heard or read, he absorbed. Moreover, both the objective and subjective essentials of good theology — revelation, experience, tradition and reason — were present. His faith unquestionably motivated him, but it was his theological understanding which directed him.

*****

Sometimes he seemed overly dependent upon the Old Testament God of Law. So, for that matter, did his peers. Nevertheless, while he would not deny an authoritative place to rules and regulations with their "Thou shalt nots," and indeed considered any violation of the Ten Commandments as flagrant sin, it was the New Testament God of Love that was central to his thinking. Not only did personal needs lead him naturally in this direction, his own capacity for affection made a less draconian deity more readily acceptable and understandable. No one who was as devoted to his children as he was, or felt the parental responsibility that he felt could fail to understand how the love of God operated.

He never used the term "Abba" — "Father,"[2] but it was a tender and watchful, caring and spiritual Father he learned to trust. The Father Jesus described as marking the sparrow's fall and numbering the hairs on his head[3] was his God. Gamaliel Bradford, one of his biographers, wrote that, "everywhere and always [Lee] had God in his heart, not so much the God of power, or the God of justice, or even the God of beauty, but the God of love. . . ."[4]

He did have a place for the "God of power" though and regularly used the word "Almighty" as a noun as well as an adjective. His early frustrations taught him the need for "The Almighty," "the God of Power and Might," and "God's almighty power." Such phrases seem artificial today, but in Lee's time North and South alike were conditioned to use them in diaries and letters and public addresses. Somehow Lee was different. He made the terms sound like expressions of awe and praise used often as synonyms for God's love.

Predictably, his thoughts about the wisdom of God showed a similar link. He used it to explain calamity but rarely without reference to the love of God which he coupled with a sense of resignation. When prospects for promotion were delayed, he explained, "We are all of us in the hand of a kind God who will do for us what is best."[5] When his hopes at the Seven Days' Battle were not totally fulfilled, he took refuge in the thought that the wisdom of God must be recognized and accepted for "God knows what is best for us."[6]

That thought always comforted him. When General "Stonewall" Jackson was mistakenly shot by his own men at Chancellorsville, Lee was plagued with the age-old question, "Why?" Yet, true to his belief he admitted that Jackson had been removed "by the hand of an inscrutable but all-wise Providence."[7] His words were almost identical in 1864 when "Jeb" Stuart was killed at Yellow Tavern. It was no different when his son Rooney was captured by the Union army, forcing him to write Mary that he would "not repine at the will of God" for he was confident that Rooney's capture would "eventuate in some good we know not now."[8] And despite the arduous retreat from Gettysburg, he was certain all would have been well had it not been for the rains which flooded the Potomac. But "God in his all-wise Providence ruled otherwise."[9]

While Lee's doubts came from grief and failures, his resolution came from understanding. He honestly believed that affliction was sometimes God's way of putting him to the test. He once said, "Human virtue should be equal to human calamity."[10] Whatever the defeat, whatever the victory, he trusted his all-wise Father in Heaven to know what was best. God's wisdom was His love once removed.

In view of his concept concerning the love of God, it seems paradoxical that his concern over Divine Justice should arouse such anxiety. Sin and retribution were very real to him, and he could only solve the dilemma which existed between God's justice and his mercy by depending upon a future compensation. As he once wrote Mary, "There is a just God in Heaven who will make all things right in time."[11]

However, God's willingness to "make all things right in time" did not imply an automatic acceptance and absolution of sin. Although Lee could not acknowledge a vengeful deity with a "terrible swift sword," neither could he accept an indulgent Father who was indifferent to His children's transgressions. As he wrote Mary shortly before Gettysburg, he could never hope Heaven would prosper their cause when they were violating God's love.[12] In another letter after Gettysburg he continued, "We must implore the forgiveness of God for our sins."[13]

General Order No. 83, issued August 13, 1863, stated "Soldier: we have sinned against Almighty God . . . and we have relied too much on our own arms for the achievement of our independence."[14] The belief that God levies a penalty for sin was a dominant factor in religious thought at that time.

Throughout the war Lee assured soldiers and civilians alike of God's continued presence, preservation and power. He promised that as long as they tried to do what was right, they could leave the outcome to Heaven without pride in victory or recrimination in defeat. He also reminded them that victory was not necessarily granted to the largest armies. Sometimes it was a reward for faith and practice, or as an instrument of Divine Justice.

Then came Appomattox. The sacred principles he believed to be the very pillars of the Southern cause were toppled, and the rights he had felt duty-bound to defend were swept away. Everything he and his people had sacrificed for and what they believed to be right had gone for naught. Where was God? How could He permit this to happen?

For many Southerners it was a shattering experience, but it was theology that steadied Lee and helped him to accept God's will. There was no pretense about understanding all the subtle interconnections between God's love and might, wisdom and justice, but in view of what he did understand Lee could console a college chaplain with the advice, again tinged with resignation, that "we have humbly tried to do our duty. We may, therefore, with calm satisfaction, trust in God and leave the rest to Him."[15]

*****

There were other aspects of Lee's theology; for example his relationship to Jesus Christ, the Son of God. The glory of Christianity, as Archbishop William Temple once wrote, is centered "not in an intellectual proposition but in a person."[16] The late Stephen Bayne described Jesus's historic ministry as "the way of the Cross, the way of Love . . . the way of sacrifice . . . the way of death, the way of beauty, the way of truth . . ." and concluded, "This is where my deep understanding of God must start."[17]

It is remarkable how neatly Lee incorporated God the Father and God the Son into his faith and doctrine. That the Son and the Father were One[18] constituted no particular problem. Words like "Christology," "Incarnation," and "Atonement" were rarely used and consequently in no need of definition. What counted was the moral standard the historic Jesus raised for a wicked world, the love He showed on a Golgotha cross, and the salvation He promised at the empty tomb. Despite all the discordant noises, in Lee's world, the words of his Father God stood loud and clear: "This is my beloved Son . . . hear ye him."[19]

Another thing Lee heard in forceful tones was the promise to provide for those who hungered and thirsted after righteousness.[20] In fact, Jesus's Sermon on the Mount set the standard for Lee's moral goodness and offered what he called "the very marrow of the Gospel."[21]

In boyhood, "Honor" had been impressed upon him as something to be coveted, earned, and protected. The word carried other connotations like "Integrity," "Honesty," and especially "Duty." Yet it remained unattached to any special aim save the rather uninspired requirement of "Being a gentleman."

Lee did not have to learn that a person could be upright as a deist, a humanist, or a believer in any number of cults. His father taught him that and prior to his maturing faith in Mexico it is possible that he traveled that road himself. It was not until he put on "the mind of Christ"[22] that his dedication to principle became bound to his faith.

Once that occurred he was protected from the common error of accepting moral and ethical integrity as the *sine qua non* of Christianity and reducing his beliefs to what Evelyn Underhill called "a bright ethical piety . . . a this world faith."[23]

However, when Jesus's teachings became joined with His divine sonship to God in Lee's mind, his moral instructions were accepted by Lee as directives from God himself. After the war in Mexico, it never occurred to Lee to doubt that. He was Christ's man first, last and always.

Lee was convinced, as his conversations and correspondence indicate, that the climax of Jesus's historical life came with His crucifixion. It should be remembered that Lee could never rid himself of an almost abnormal conviction of his unworthiness. When this was combined with his additional belief that adversity sometimes came as a test, it is no wonder that he wanted a Savior to commit to more than a moral example. Belief in his sinfulness drove him to Christ to ask for forgiveness and redemption. It caused him to remember promises like "he saved his people from their sin,"[24] "neither do I condemn thee; go and sin no more,"[25] and the first words from the cross "Father, forgive them, for they know not what they do."[26] And it also prompted his overly active conscience to pray fervently for redemption.

Reluctant though he was about publicizing such feelings, occasionally he made exceptions. The Rev. J. William Jones reported that at times Lee's eyes would shine and his voice would ring as he told of his need for the redeeming Christ. He had no hesitancy in admitting to the Reverend B. F. Lacy that he was "nothing but a poor sinner, trusting in Christ alone for salvation."[27]

He reasoned that moral behavior by itself could not earn Heaven. Only the salvation which Christ bestowed could do that. So the weight of his prayers for his family, his men, and the students at Washington College lay in that direction and spurred unprecedented messages to those in his charge to humble *themselves* before God and pray in Christ's name for the forgiveness of their sins.[28]

Had a request for purity and humility been issued by a Napoleon or Wellington that would have seemed absurd, but such requests were so characteristic of Lee's fatherly concern for his young unprofessional troops that they aroused neither resentment nor ridicule. In fact, his men knew he applied such calls to himself and felt even closer to him because of them.

During the Reconstruction period as well as the war years, the Christ of the Cross was never far from Lee's mind. The atonement the Cross promised was the assurance that his feeling of unworthiness required, and he had no hesitancy in passing the good news on to all for whom he felt any sense of responsibility. Lee doubtless was familiar with C. F. Alexander's words which were put to music in 1844.

> There is a green hill far away
> Without the city wall,
> Where the dear Lord was crucified
> Who died to save us all.[29]

Lee taught this, promised it, and it is little wonder that he tied this salient belief in the cross to an Eastern faith which viewed mortality as a preface to eternity. When his daughter, Annie, died he struggled free from an almost overwhelming despair and comforted Mary with an assurance of God's everlasting Kingdom and the assurance that their child had been taken "at a time and place when it was best for her to go."[30] Humility then joined consolation as he expressed the hope that when their lives were needed they would be as ready for the summons as she had been.

His son, Rooney, was still locked in a Union prison when his wife, Charlotte, died, and again his father was forced to bury personal sorrow in order to assuage Mary's grief with the reminder that her sorrow was a prologue to eventual joy. A note of hopelessness is detectable in an additional statement that all their family ties were being broken link by link, then quickly balanced by the thought that their own passage to the next world would be smoothed by loved ones who had gone before and that some day they would all be reunited in a Heaven of rest.

Of course, Lee knew that Jesus's promise of love, peace, and strength applied as readily to this world as the next, but inasmuch as he had not received them in any great measure, he became more and more positive that triumph over tribulation and enjoyment of peace were, for the most part, held in store for the next life. In this, he was an A.D. man who gave scant place to B.C. hopes.

Nowhere was this more apparent than in the letters of condolence he addressed to hundreds in their sorrow. He complained that his efforts were painfully difficult because of his inadequacy with words, but his faith and compassion always shone through and to this day his letters serve as models of faith and belief and compassion to those who mourn.

When his cherished friend, George W. Randolph, died he counseled Mrs. Randolph with the explanation that her husband had been called to receive his reward for a life of righteousness. On the death of Mac Moses Hoge he sent a gentle reminder to her husband, the Reverend Dr. Hoge of Richmond's Second Presbyterian Church, that God's infinite mercy and power are never more available than in times of sorrow. In a letter written the final year of his life to Samuel R. George of Baltimore, he summed up his thoughts, saying, "The great God of heaven takes us at the period when it is best for us to go . . . Every beat of our hearts marks our progress . . . towards the grave."[31]

Such expressions were not pious platitudes. They rang with the vibrant conviction of a man totally committed to a Risen Lord, whose followers would "not perish but have everlasting life."[32] Lee was not morbidly preoccupied with death; he saw it as a natural event which would summon him in due time as it did all mortals. These constant experiences with death reinforced his belief in the "now" as a prelude to the "then" and made the promise of life everlasting a supreme factor in his theology.

Together with most church people of his day, he believed that Heaven was a literal dwelling place. It had a specific "up there" location and was populated with all the redeemed throughout the ages. This belief was too real for the grave to hold any terror for him. Death was a sad event for those who were left behind to mourn; otherwise, it was small thing when compared to the glorious life to come.

In all, Lee's theology led him to understand the Jesus of history who taught, healed, and loved. It also clarified the Christ of eternity who forgave, redeemed, and promised everlasting life. And it helped him to see that he could walk in the light of his Lord's presence no matter how great the surrounding darkness.

*****

Although Lee's few thoughts about the Holy Spirit were equally orthodox, like most mid-nineteenth century Christians, he seemed more inclined to center his faith on the first two Persons of the Trinity and to neglect what Bible and prayer book taught about the Holy Spirit, the Comforter.

Surely he was familiar with his Lord's promise to send the Comforter[33] and the description of Him as "The Spirit of Truth."[34] Nor could anyone as diligent in Bible reading as he was have failed to be affected by the Pentecostal Upper Room experience and the Spirit's descent like tongues of fire.[35] He could not have been unaware of the Catechism's distinction between "God the Father who hath made me" (past tense), "God the Son who hath redeemed me" (past tense), and "God the Holy Ghost who sanctifieth me ..." (present tense.)[36] The Third Person of the Trinity has always been described as "The Present Tense of God."

The Nicene Creed recites, "And I believe in the Holy Ghost, the Lord and Giver of Life, who proceedeth from the Father and the Son" ... (and) "who spoke by the Prophets."[37] The Order of Confirmation contained a prayer which goes further and listed the seven-fold gifts of the Holy Spirit: "... the Spirit of wisdom and understanding, the spirit of counsel and ghostly strength, the spirit of knowledge and true godliness, ... and ... the spirit of thy holy fear."[38]

Of course, there were instances when he became enthusiastic about the Spirit's operation. Bishop Joseph Wilmer of Louisiana in an address following Lee's death related that Lee's countenance glowed and his voice rang in response when the bishop stated that "the Holy Spirit was the great Teacher whose presence was required if education was to be a blessing and not a curse."[39] The Reverend J. William Jones once insisted that the success of a campus revival must depend on the Holy Spirit and reported that Lee became emotional in agreement.[40] It was also Jones who recounted a conversation that when speaking of the Bible, Lee confessed there were many things he might not be able to explain in it, but that he accepted it "as the infallible word of God and received its teachings as inspired by the Holy Ghost."[41]

Thus he was quick to admit the Holy Spirit's power, but he rarely spoke or wrote of its influence over his personal life. The probable reason for this is that he failed to draw a distinction between Christ and the Comforter.

*****

Lee was far more definite about the Doctrine of Man. As a boy and young man his consideration of and care for others were unrelated to any philosophy or theology. Parental training taught him respect for every sort and condition of human being. This grew into "A Gentleman's Code of Courtesy" with a knowledge of the dignity of each and every person. But a maturing faith provided a totally different scale for the measurement of human beings.

It was his understanding of the fatherhood of God which made it possible to believe in the human community. St. Luke's Gospel pictured the extent to which God as the Shepherd was willing to go in search of his lost sheep, the housewife would search for her lost coin, and the father would welcome his prodigal son.[42] No human being could be judged inferior where in the eyes of God he was valued so highly. A slave, a stable boy, and even a rascal were unique and precious in God's sight, and brotherly love went far deeper than obligation, or patronage, or reluctant acceptance.[43] The easy rapport which Lee had with the common soldier and the manner in which he began to act out the "Love Ethic" with forgiveness, kindness, service, and equality to all are sufficient evidence.

An unusual letter written against the background of the Reconstruction period and addressed to his former aide, Colonel Charles Marshall, contained some conclusions which have been published since under the title of "A Faith." The designation is apt to be misleading since Lee's remarks are more philosophical than theological, but in the shadow of their philosophy stands his staunch belief in the ultimate goodness of people. In part it reads:

> My experience of men has never disposed me to think more of them, nor indisposed me to serve them; Nor, in spite of failures which I lament, or the present, aspect of affairs, do I despair the future.[44]

Neither the vengeful natures of a few political leaders in the North, nor the retaliating attempts by their counterparts in the South could dispose him to think any less of his fellow man. While admitting "the fault and corruption of the nature of every man,"[45] he also believed that for the repentant the Atoning Christ equalized that original sin with His Cross.

It has already been noted that it is not customary for military commanders, past or present, to request prayers for the conversion of the enemy. That, however, is precisely what Lee did on more than one occasion. College presidents are not prone to make the spirituality of their students a first priority, but Lee did, saying wistfully, "If only I could know that all young men in this college were good Christians."[46] It is true that in his day people talked more willingly about God, but few did so with the same underlying belief in a single person's value in the eyes of God.

CHAPTER SEVEN

To Do What Is Right!

Not the least of Lee's accomplishments was his victory over himself. Before he was twelve years old a vague inner prompting was urging him to perfection. By the time he entered the U.S. Military Academy family and friends had whetted his appetite for high moral standards and pointed him to the value of a living faith. When faith entered his life, its fruits transferred him into a classic example of what a Christian ought to be. It taught him that goodness could not be achieved in a vacuum and that, as Dag Hammarskjold confessed, "The road to Holiness necessarily passes through the world of action."[1] Thus the sword of righteousness which was cast by his parents in childhood became his tool against incessant temptation.

Two months after Appomattox with the ashes of defeat surrounding him and the premonition of death hovering over him, he penned a letter to his good friend, Mrs. Martha ("Markie") Williams, in which he summarized the guiding goal of his life: "I have always endeavored to do what is right."[2] Upon that declaration he rested his reputation.

*****

One's self-respect was as sacred in the South during the nineteenth century as it was in Victorian England. Young men of Lee's day learned to wear their reputations like a knight's plume, to wear it proudly, guard it jealously, and give it a spiritual quality which polished up their manners. This concept among Virginia's elite was inherited from forebears who had raised them in the Biblical tradition that "a good name is rather to be chosen than great riches."[3]

Pride in his good name came early to Lee but earlier still came an arrogant and stubborn streak which concerned his mother so greatly that she wrote her sister, Elizabeth Randolph, for advice. Elizabeth replied that if Robert was proving difficult to manage, the only advice she had to give was to practice that which she employed with her own son, namely to "whip and pray and pray and whip."[4]

While Ann Lee was no doubt prepared to follow such counsel, there is no evidence that she was forced to do so. Apparently her prayers, her love, and her example sufficed for as he matured, young Lee began to pattern his life after hers. This was bolstered by the circumstance of his father's blackened reputation. Ann preserved correspondence from Lighthorse Harry addressed to Carter, Robert's older brother. For example, it was to Carter he wrote that he would rather him be unlettered and untutored "if virtuous."[5] Ann created a fireside atmosphere in the home. There, with devout ceremony, she pictured her absent husband as a national hero and a paragon of virtue. Little wonder therefore that Harry's advice on virtue became an imperative.

There was always Lee's other hero, George Washington. The only fear that truly frightened the first president was a fear of losing his honor.[6] That which motivated him was his conviction that to defend what was right could never be wrong. Loyal friends were fond of saying, "He simply could not be as high a man as he was believed to be—but he was."[7]

Lee did not receive a single demerit at West Point and graduated second in the Class of 1829 (his son, Custis, was to graduate at the top of his class twenty-five years later), with a grade of 300 out of 300 in conduct and 1,966 1/2 out of 2,000 in general merit. Having also concluded while at the Academy that the use of tobacco, alcohol, and barrack-room profanity were not only threats to self-discipline but proof of the loss of it, he determined to abstain from these temptations for the rest of his life.

Surprisingly, his student peers were neither jealous of his attainments nor scornful of his rigid moral discipline. Sir Galahads are not generally popular on school campuses. Their impeccable behavior as model students is far more acceptable to the faculty than to their fellow students. But while the cadets were somewhat in awe of Lee and called him "Marble Lee," as much for his dignified behavior as for his handsome looks, they could not deny that he was a man's man or denigrate his attention to duty and discipline.

His regulated life had stern and exacting qualities. Among them were personal neatness, a love of orderliness, a strict punctuality, and a frugality which permitted no costlier purchase than his purse could afford. In years to come his wife would reveal that his passion for orderliness made it possible for him to enter a pitch-black room and lay his hand on a particular paper or article of clothing without difficulty. Along with family prayers, he was insistent on promptness at church services as well as to every engagement. His children remarked how on more than one occasion he departed, leaving his tardy wife to follow. While he obviously enjoyed the physical comfort of Arlington, he taught himself to accept the meager fare and plain surroundings of a soldier with such ease that few were conscious of the marked contrast between his civilian and his military life. Manifestly, his father's financial ineptness was responsible for the conviction that living within one's means would save anxiety and mortification.

The examples of his self-control are abundant. Because he saw the difficulties others were having with alcohol he chose to abstain. When the army's medical director recommended port wine as an antidote to a debilitating illness and sent him a case, he refused to open it. Neither did he use tobacco in any form. And though he was raised in an environment where horse racing and card playing were common amusements he refused politely to engage. His strictness in money matters had such a firm moral base that even in the midst of war he sent two one dollar gold pieces through the lines in payment for a forgotten Arlington debt with a note of apology to a Washington resident. With food so scarce during the conflict, on the rare occasions when good meat was available he refused a second helping and disguised his consideration for his hostess saying, "I should really enjoy another piece but I've had my allowance."[8]

There is no recorded instance when his conversations in the field or barracks could not have been equally acceptable in a lady's drawing room. An examination of the two thousand letters which still exist fails to uncover the slightest suggestion of vulgarity. Sometimes his distaste for coarseness was so embarrassing to those of less disciplined tongue that they would react as General Henry A. Wise did on one occasion, protesting, "I am perfectly willing that Jackson and yourself shall do the praying for the whole Army of Northern Virginia; but, in Heaven's name, let me do the cussin' for one small brigade."[9]

Anger and depression were among his chief frailties and, understandably, called for continued self-discipline. A case in point was the word exchange he had with President Jefferson Davis towards the end of the war. He was fighting frantically to hold a sagging line before Petersburg when he received a curt wire from the president demanding that he drop everything and come to Richmond to discuss some rumors which were circulating in the area. Lee felt his military situation was too risky to absent himself and with unaccustomed exasperation answered, "Send me the measures and I will send you my views." Davis, who doubtless had pressures of his own, also lost his temper and sent a hot reply assuring Lee that his counsel would not be needed. Quietly, Lee made his way to Richmond and several days later wrote a conciliatory letter to the president.[10]

However, whenever correction of military subordinates or college students became necessary, he strove first of all to be in command of himself. He did not raise his voice or pound on the desk or threaten, yet with quiet emphasis and sometimes with humor he left the offender in no doubt of his requirements. The glove was velvet but the hand was steel.

During the siege of Petersburg, he once asked whether the defensive works he had ordered were completed. When the officer in charge hesitated before answering affirmatively, Lee proposed a visit to the sector where he found little had been done. When his embarrassed companion admitted he had not inspected the works personally, Lee did not reply directly. Instead he turned to admire the officer's mount and when learning the animal belonged to his wife suggested, "I would urge you to take some of the mettle out of him."

Along with knowing oneself comes preparing oneself, and in this connection Lee had a unique manner of preparation. Apart from Holy Scripture which was ever his chief teacher and guide, he began the accumulation of little notes on moral and ethical subjects which he filed away for future use. Some were original; many were unidentified quotations. All served as an aid to virtue and a defense against bigotry.

A reference which sounds especially like him argues that "Honesty in its widest sense is always honorable. The trite sayings that 'Honesty is the best policy' has met with the just criticism that honesty is not a policy. This seems to be true. The real honest man is honest from conviction of what is right, not from policy."[11] Such a statement could have come straight from the heart of his moral convictions.

On the other hand, when Edward Valentine, the sculptor, expressed regret over the large material losses Lee had sustained because of the war, he answered quietly, "Misfortune nobly borne is good fortune." At the time Valentine was impressed by what he thought was an original observation only to discover later that it was a quotation from *The Meditations of Marcus Aurelius.*[12]

At his death his old military satchel was found to contain a number of these moral pronouncements: preachments and moral stories for public use as well as personal benefit. Combined, they bear a strong resemblance to the Old Testament's Book of Proverbs and like the ancient wisdom literature, they are pragmatic, not speculative or abstract, and they unite a homespun wisdom with a moral intelligence in pointing the way "to the good life. Many of them have been preserved in General Long's *Memoirs of Robert E. Lee.*

Lee emphasized the need for understanding when there are differences of opinion and advised putting one's self in the other person's shoes. "Those who oppose our purpose are always to be regarded as our enemies. We usually think and act from our immediate surroundings. . . . The better rule is to judge our adversaries from their standpoint, not from ours. God disposes. This ought to satisfy us."[13]

To the old adage that "Charity should begin at home," he insisted that all limitations should be removed, saying, "Charity should have no beginning or ending."[14]

Frequent separations from his children and the suspicion that Mrs. Lee was too lenient with them caused him to sprinkle an unusual number of single sentence directives for their benefit through his correspondence.

As they matured his advice was aimed directly at them. One which was written to his son, Custis, probably when he was in his teens, has all the tone of Shakespeare's Polonius giving advice to his son. The letter lists what Lee believed to be the essential qualities of successful living: "study to be frank with the world; frankness is the child of honesty and courage;" "never do a wrong thing to make a friend or keep one;" "do not appear to others what you are not;" "there is no more dangerous experiment than that of undertaking to be one thing before a man's face and another behind his back;" "we should live, act, and say nothing to the injury of any one."[15]

His daughter, Mildred, was shown a three-fold way to the good life in a letter written from camp near Petersburg on November 1, 1864. "Habituate yourself to useful employment, regular improvement, and to the benefit of all those around you."[16]

To "Tabb," Rooney's new wife, he wrote: "I hope . . . you are becoming more and more interested in making those around you happy . . . This is the true way to secure your own happiness."[17]

With sadness on every side, he also evidenced a belief in the modern equivalent, "Show your wounds only to the doctor," by offering the following advice to his cousin, Mrs. Anna Fitzhugh: "A man may manifest and communicate his joy, but he should conceal and smother his grief as much as possible."[18]

"Markie" Williams, who he considered one of the family, also came in for her share of advice. "That virtue is worth but little that requires constant watching and removal from temptation."[19] "There is scarcely anything that is right that we cannot hope to accomplish by labor and perseverance. But the first must be earnest and the second unremitting."[20]

One of his most strongly held convictions was expressed at one time or another to each member of the family. "If you want to be missed by your friends, be useful."[21]

A young Lexington mother who sought a blessing for her son in the Biblical tradition was told simply: "Teach him to deny himself."[22]

He had no more important advice to offer than that which was given a small namesake. "Above all things, learn at once to worship your Creator and to do His Holy Will as revealed in His Holy Book."[23]

When a West Point cadet fell so far behind in his work that it was obvious he could not pass a coming examination, Lee suggested with a parent's understanding that the father withdraw his son and save him the embarrassment of failing. He hastened to add, however: "I consider the character of no man affected by a want of success provided he has made an honest effort to succeed."[24]

And as an aid to his ministry of reconciliation after the war, as well as a reminder to his students, he stressed over and over that: "Obedience to lawful authority is the foundation of manly character."[25]

*****

Holy Scripture reminds that "as (a man) thinketh in his heart so is he,"[26] and the acquired virtues which shaped the goodness of Robert Lee were assuredly born from the beliefs of his heart. Others in his day spoke as he spoke; but the proof of his faith lay not in what he said, but in what he did and what he was. His character verified his communications.

Lee's efforts at moral and ethical conduct were best expressed by the words of a simple soldier engaged in a campfire discussion of Charles Darwin's theory of evolution. He spoke for every man in the army when he said to his companions, "Well, boys, the rest of us may have *developed* from monkeys; but I tell you *none less than God could have made such a man as 'Marse Robert!'*"[27] He may not have reached the unsophisticated level of a Brother Lawrence, but like that saintly Carmelite monk he discovered the little cell within his soul to which he could retire from his hostile world and be alone with his Lord. And because he had so successfully geared his will to God's will, again like Brother Lawrence, he could interpret the simplest event as divinely inspired. He sounded precisely like the gentle monk when he wrote Agnes from Fredericksburg of the cold, sullen rain he was enduring and added with humor but in all sincerity, "See how kind God is; we have plenty to do in good weather and bad."[28]

The similarity is even more pronounced in his refusal to be troubled by doctrinal dilemmas and theological disputes. Jesus said, "Except ye be converted and become as little children, ye shall not enter the kingdom of Heaven."[29] The simplicity of Lee's faith corresponded to that of Brother Lawrence in this respect as well for neither could be swayed from their course by the winds of controversy. Both responded to Christ with the awe and reverence and innocence of little children.

That innocence included self-confidence. "God's will be done" was not a grudging submission to a Will which he believed to be less desirable than his own. As Archbishop William Temple wrote, "That would have been blasphemous."[30] He saw God as the Prime Mover of all events and therefore was confident of ultimate victory.

To President Davis during the anxious days of December 1864, or to his wife on hearing of his daughter-in-law Charlotte's death, or in his military plans, there was always a "God will cause all things to work together for good."[31] Not only did his confidence move him to see history at close range with expectation, but it undergirded the strategy he employed in pitting his diminishing army against the numerically superior and magnificently equipped foe. Readying him for long-range issues, this confidence provided the ultimate optimism in his ministry of reconciliation after the war. Colonel Garnet Wolsely of England, later Field Marshal Viscount Wolsely, described him to perfection as a man ". . . confident of ultimate success under the blessings of the Almighty, whom he glorified for past successes, and whom he invoked for all future operations."[32]

Then with confidence leading, patience followed automatically as another outgrowth of his faith. Together they at least minimized the depression of spirit which misfortune created. When he spoke of a resignation to God's will, he was not only expressing a submissive acceptance of whatever God had ordained, but the forbearance necessary to await God's ultimate victory. It was never a hopeless acceptance of tribulation which had the final say, but a solid conviction that some day, in this world or in the next, all inequalities would be made right and he had only to wait. That was what saved him many times with President Davis. It steadied him when his lieutenant failed to carry out his orders. And it protected him against temptation to react publicly to General Joe Johnston's ambition, General Longstreet's temperament, and General Jackson's lack of diplomacy with his subordinates.

Convinced though Lee was that his times were in the hands of God, that fact did not blind him to an understanding that God often waits to help those who will help themselves. Accordingly, while confidence grew out of his trust in God's ultimate victory, patience kept his chosen goals in sight. Often it took persistence to produce the final results. As his nephew, General Fitzhugh Lee, described him: "Always cool, sagacious, resolute, reliant, he was never at loss for expedients, never disturbed by unforeseen accidents, never without a clear conception of the objects to be achieved; and the best way of achieving it."[33]

An active sense of responsibility made him determined to teach self-control to his children and especially to his sons. In an early letter to Mary he voiced the same objection to Custis' self-will and obstancy that his mother had once made of his. "[I]t is our duty, if possible, to counteract them and assist him to bring them under his control," he wrote. "[A]nd we must endeavor to combine the mildness and forbearance of the mother with the sternness and, perhaps, unreasonableness of the father."[34] Another letter advised, "You must not let him run wild in my absence and will have to exercise firm authority over all of them."[35] His action to Rooney on strictness in money matters is a classic. "It is easier to make our wishes conform to our means," he explained, "than to make our means conform to our wishes." His son, Rob, recalled that as a small boy he was required to police his room, pass a military-like inspection, and render unquestioning obedience. Looking back, he spoke for his brothers and sisters as well when he said, "All the roads of life were carefully worked out for us."[36]

As with their character, so with their conduct. Even when his sons were grown men wearing Confederate uniforms, Lee continued to show anxiety over their behavior and concern for the example they were setting. In January of 1864 when the general deterioration of Southern fortunes were beginning to be all too apparent, a festive ball was planned at Charlottesville, perhaps with a thought to the morale of the young officers who were in winter quarters there. Lee, however, disapproved of such gaiety in the midst of widespread suffering, and the fact that his sons and nephew were involved was a source of embarrassment. So with parental bluntness he picked up his pen to write: "There are too many Lees on the committee. I like them to be present for battles, but can excuse them from balls."[37]

Determination and patience, yes, but was there a deeper power from which they were derived? Were parental directions, the persuasive Washington influence, and one short course in moral philosophy at the military academy enough? On the surface it would seem so for there is no evidence that he borrowed any religious books from the library during his four years at West Point, or engaged in any special search for spiritual assistance. Yet as with Paul "kicking against the pricks," Augustine with his mistress, Francis of Assisi enjoying his comfortable life as a rich man's son, and all the others who in their early years seemed indifferent to God, the Holy Spirit was unquestionably at work in Lee to provide whatever was necessary for the future. It was not genes, nor parental example, nor hero worship, but the Spirit of God that was responsible for empowering and guiding him.

*****

The components of Lee's drive for a stout character and especially the offshoots of his faith made him one of history's most conspicuous examples of a good man in an evil world. As an unending victim of adversity, he donned the whole armor of God and to paraphrase Paul, withstood the evil day.[38] General Gordon noted in retrospect that his former commander's performance was a living rebuke to a remark attributed to the Duke of Wellington that "A man of fine Christian sensibilities is totally unfit for the position of a soldier."[39] Shortly after his death his wife wrote, "I have never so truly felt the purity of his character as now...."[40]

CHAPTER EIGHT

Character

A casual glance at the life of Robert E. Lee confirms T. S. Eliot's observation that as a thinking man's faith is, so will his morals be.[1] As faith took control, supportive virtues were developed which made him a classic example of Christian character. No "Compromise Ethic" was a factor here; no surrender of a few moral convictions was even considered. By his faith he was free to seek righteousness and make it the unrestricted aim of his life.

It did not take long for him to realize, however, that goodness cannot be exercised in a vacuum. Thus, while the sword of Lee's righteousness was cast in his childhood and fashioned by the romanticism of his age, it was honed on the grindstone of stern reality and used day after day against constant temptation. That is one of the primary reasons he is admired as much for his struggle to become a practicing Christian as for his secular accomplishments. Not the least of his victories was the victory over himself.

Lee was as concerned with correct conduct as the vain young Pharisee of the parable, but he possessed a different set of values.[2] The code of a gentleman which would not permit such vanity was reinforced by a spirituality which saw all men, whatever the state of their sinfulness, as brother. No one who had stood so often in the presence of his Creator and received what he believed to be undeserved forgiveness could fail to acknowledge the dignity and worth of God's other created beings. At the same time he never for a moment pretended that his achievements were the product of personal talent. Always, they were the result of God working in him and through him. As General A. L. Long remarked in a somewhat wordy sentence: "The Christian character of General Lee was one in which the tenderness, forgiveness, philanthropy, and purity of the real disciple of the true Christ conception were the ruling impulses and not the haughty, austere self-satisfaction or the unrelenting exacting creed of those who consider themselves elect."[3]

That is why he could remain unaffected by public plaudits and in all honesty never understand people's adulation. It was no pose. Why they made such a fuss over him after his return to civilian life was forever a mystery. His greatest embarrassment, had he lived, would have been to hear and read what his biographers wrote about him. His modesty never failed to inspire the love of the youngest child and hardiest veteran.

During the war he rarely wore a dress uniform or the proper insignia of his rank and was apt to content himself with a colonel's stars. When one of his men remarked on this he replied, "I do not care for display . . . the truth is, that the rank of colonel is about as high as I ought ever to have gotten."[4] From the moment he stood in the halls of Virginia's state capitol and told those who had given him command of the state's military forces that he would have preferred their choice to have fallen on an abler man to his retirement in Lexington where secretly at night he gathered up and shined the shoes his guests had left outside their doors for non-existent servants, Lee's lack of pride was his most endearing asset. He took everyone seriously except himself.

This acute sense of unworthiness also caused a rejection of people's "golden opinion." After the battles of Seven Days, Second Manassas, Fredericksburg, and Chancellorsville, he gave credit where he sincerely believed credit was due, saying to Mary Lee as his popularity mounted, "I tremble for my country when I hear the confidence expressed in me. I know too well my weaknesses and that our only hope is in God."[5] When the Richmond City Council proposed to purchase his home for him as a mark of gratitude, he told Mary, "It causes me to reflect how little I have done to merit it and humbles me in my own eyes to a painful degree."[6] His modesty was suitably described after the Battle of Chancellorsville when one of his officers was asked, "Does it make the General proud to see how his men love him?" "Not proud," the officer replied. "It awes him."[7]

His aide, Col. Charles Marshall, maintained that military reports always underrated his part in the engagements and on more than one occasion, as at Gettysburg, "covered the errors and omissions of all his officers." They contained, Marshall said, "an utter forgetfulness of self, that made me lose my admiration of the great soldier in my reverence for the excellence of the man."[8]

His counterpart in the Union army often offered a telling contrast. General George McClellan had little difficulty in becoming a hero to himself, and in believing what was being said and written about him as "the Little Napoleon." In a letter to his wife he boasted, "The President, cabinet, General Scott, and all (are) deferring to me . . . I seem to have become a power in the land."[9] Whereupon he began to advise President Lincoln on national political issues as well as on the conduct of the war. But at the same time he could not capture the Confederate's capital. Union General John Pope's soaring ambition priced him out of his class. With inordinate self-importance about his new appointment as commander, he issued a General Order saying, "I have come from the West, where we have always seen the backs of our enemies . . . I hear constantly of 'taking strong positions and holding them,' 'lines of retreat,' and 'bases of supplies.'" Let us discard such ideas . . . Let us study the probable line of retreat of our enemies, and leave our own to take care of themselves"[10] But that was before Second Manassas. He was followed by "Fighting Joe Hooker" who looked at the mirror on the wall and saw the finest soldier of them all. After the First Battle of Manassas, he boldly informed the president, "I'm a damned sight better general than you had on that field"; and when given the opportunity to prove it, scorned the failures of his predecessors with the confident prophecy, "When I get to Richmond."[11] However, he never got past Chancellorsville!

It is interesting to note that the greatest criticism of Lee's military leadership lies in this same area of his humility. The prerogative of a commander is to order: "Do this," "Attack there," "Defend here," and it is the duty of his troops to obey without question. Lee, however, was famous for such orders as, "You must act according to your best judgment . . . ," "If you agree . . . ,"and "Should you find it advisable . . ." With Stonewall Jackson, and to a degree Jeb Stuart, this was all that was necessary, but other commanders could not perform under such latitude. Some required more explicit orders, others a firmer hand if they were not to take advantage, but to Lee dictatorship, even the necessary dictatorship of a commanding officer, was an impossibility. There was an inner compulsion to pay his corps and division commanders the compliment of trusting their modesty, their loyalty, and their ability.

The same lack of vaulting ego was carried into his person-to-person relationships with officers and men. Once when he was considering a certain officer for promotion, some members of his staff objected on the grounds that the man had been sharply critical of him. Lee replied quietly that it was not the officer's opinion of him which was under discussion, but his opinion of the officer. The promotion went through.

A number of commonplace incidents, rarely mentioned, which took place after his retirement also illustrate Lee's lack of egotism. Mary Lee was not purposely domineering, but in her illness she did not always realize how she ordered her husband about as though he were a little child. The former commanding officer whose orders had moved hundreds of thousands would hasten to do her bidding as though fearful of being sent to bed without his supper. He sat uncomplainingly when she decided to trim his hair, ran on command to locate a misplaced hat of a young visitor, and dutifully brought her meals and medicines at their appointed times. It never occurred to him to think that he was too important for such menial tasks. A reminder perhaps of the saying that "he who believes he is too big to do little things, is in reality too little to do big things."

One exception to Lee's normal meekness was his attitude towards photographers. As his son, Rob, pointed out, there is no representation which truly captures his gentle disposition for he considered posing for a photograph or portrait so serious a matter he could never completely relax. An uncomfortable self-consciousness crept over him which the honesty of the camera rarely failed to reveal, and on not a few occasions a slight irritation and even sternness resulted from having to conform strictly to the dictates of the photographers. Matthew Brady caught such an expression in his familiar pictures taken at the rear of Lee's Franklin Street residence in Richmond shortly after Appomattox.

Another exception often resulted when strangers were persistent in requesting a photograph. He could not believe anyone could honestly want a picture of such a "grizzly old veteran" and was apt to become ill-humored over frequent petitions. When his friend, Markie Williams, requested a description of Traveler, he wrote detailed pages in reply. But he could never see himself as other than a balding, be-whiskered "antique" whose image was not worth preserving.

The successful transition he made from military life to the new one at Washington College was also due in no small degree to modesty. The past might easily have created deep resentments, dark depressions and oppressive longings by a constant review of former achievements and honors, but, again, his lack of an inflated ego was his salvation. He cast off his military exploits with a wave of the hand and, save for an occasional remark concerning the suffering and grief of Southern people, refused to discuss the past.[12]

In those days he wore his old campaign hat and parts of Confederate gray uniform with the insignia removed as most veterans were doing for economy's sake. There was nothing but his bearing to distinguish him from other service men and that was the way he wanted it. He never forgot the past with its horrors and its heroisms, but he buried it deep inside in deference to what he considered to be God's call to Lexington. Never did he offer the slightest evidence of measuring what may now have seemed a prosaic existence with his former dramatic life, or of shaking his fist at Heaven in regret.

Of course, in his day the character of every Virginia gentleman was expected to reflect a modest behavior, and he was taught from early childhood to see that it did. But too often the very teaching caused landed aristocrats to assume an arrogance which could not be disguised. Something more than family training was necessary if they were to become the gentlemen they were expected to become.

In Lee's case, a regimen of Bible reading and study left him in no doubt of the emphasis Christianity placed on its virtue. There were innumerable texts and personal illustrations, all leading from Paul's statement that "Charity (Love) . . . vaunteth not itself, is not puffed up,"[13] and especially Jesus' command, "Take my yoke upon you and learn of me; for I am meek and lowly of heart."[14] This created the stimuli which made for authentic modesty.

But Lee had another defense against pride—his sense of humor.

Major Heros Von Brocke, a German officer of gigantic physical proportions who served as an aide to General Stuart, was erroneously reported to have been killed at Chancellorsville and permission was requested of Lee for his body to be moved to Richmond where it could lie in state at the Capitol. Since the major was not dead, but on a cavalry raid at the time, Lee reported solemnly, "[I] can't spare it! It's in pursuit of [Union General] Stoneman!"[15]

When Sweeny, General Stuart's celebrated banjo player, was serenading a group of officers near Lee's tent one evening, he came out to thank the musician and observed a jug of rye whiskey sitting nearby. "Gentlemen," he remarked with twinkling eyes, "am I to thank General Stuart or the jug for this fine music?"[16]

He was no prude and often took pleasure in teasing others about their deficiencies. One day he asked several of his staff if they would "like a glass of something." Having seen a bottle of brandy in his tent, which, incidentally, he carried through the war unopened, they accepted with alacrity. Calling Bryan, his mess steward, he had glasses distributed ceremoniously as the men gathered eagerly about the table, then he poured into each glass—buttermilk! The staff dared not refuse and his amusement mounted as they put their best foot forward and gulped it down dutifully.[17]

He never joked with people he did not like, and General J. B. Hood was one officer he especially delighted in teasing. Once when the commander of the famous Texas Brigade came to visit, he found Lee discussing the problem of pilfering in the army with Colonel Chilton. Hood immediately protested the innocence of his own men, and Lee did not contradict him. He simply smiled sweetly and said, "Ah, General Hood, when you Texans come about the chickens have to roost mighty high."[18]

No one could blush like Stonewall Jackson, however, and Lee could never resist the opportunity to make his brilliant general uncomfortable in the presence of admirers, particularly young lady admirers, by giving exaggerated and even fanciful accounts of Jackson's exploits. Then he would step back with undisguised glee while Jackson with eyes downcast began to shuffle his feet, or twitch in his saddle, as his face turned a deeper shade of red.

Most of all he loved bantering with young people. During his stay at Fort Hamilton he wrote Markie Williams a description of the love-bitten young men at the base, calling them heroes who were poised high on the wings of love, when gazing at the "Divinities" of their worship. But, he added, though as soldiers they struck like falcons, in courting they wooed like turtles.[19] He also told her that son Rooney had appropriated the room she had used during a recent visit and turned it into a study. This meant, he explained, "It must, therefore, be considered vacant."[20] Writing from Mexico during the summer of 1848, with mock gravity he urged that a certain young lady be admonished for her interest in a clergyman. She should take care to marry a soldier, he advised, and never a clergyman. There was always the possibility that a soldier might be shot, but it would take a special dispensation from Providence to get rid of a young minister.[21]

Newspaper editors, or "newspaper generals" as he termed them, who delighted in second guessing military strategy were special subjects of his barbed wit. This is illustrated by a statement to Hon. B. H. Hill: "We made a great mistake, Mr. Hill, in the beginning of our struggle, and I fear, in spite of all we can do it will prove to be a fatal mistake . . . we appointed all our worst generals to command the armies, and all our best generals to edit the newspapers."[22] Conceit could also spur biting remarks. When one of his officers criticized an associate, not without truth, Lee answered formally, "Well, Sir, if that is your impression of General — — —, I can only say that you differ widely from the General's opinion of himself."[23]

*****

Dr. Marshall W. Fishwick described Lee's sense of duty in almost religious terms: "Duty was more than a principle to Robert E. Lee. It was a ritual."[24] To the extent that it promoted good works and compassionate sensitivity, it assuredly was. In fact, Lee's faith and unending quest for righteousness elevated his moral responsibility to the level of a ministry. General A. L. Long had the insight to see this. He called it the instinct of a Christian soldier who desired to devote his life to the attainment of "high impersonal ends, and whose ambition was to serve."[25]

This ambition to serve continued to develop over the years until it became a dominate reason for doing his duty. Love, of course, was inextricably bound to it. The first incentive of duty and love came when he was his mother's "outdoor agent and confidential messenger,"[26] as well as a constant attendant for his infant sister Mildred, and the sickly Anne. As he grew older, the examples of others began to register and, quite naturally, none did so more forcibly than "the great Washington" whose compassion for others was as legendary as his self-control. It took, however, the spiritual growth inherent in later years and especially its new power of unfaltering love to make a virtue of service and lift it above the level of impersonal benevolence.

Manifestly, the pleasure Lee derived from performing his obligations could neither erase the pain and misery it sometimes caused, nor restore the toll it took upon his body, mind, and spirit. It would be an exaggeration to say he went to his grave with a broken heart, for his faith was too strong for that. But it is undeniably true that the taxing burden of memory was never relieved by the satisfaction of knowing he had done his duty as God had given him to see it. Over and over, his friends, and particularly his young friends, remarked on the sadness that so often characterized him after the war. He knew full well that allegiance to obligation does not necessarily produce self-content.

*****

At Arlington, the children soon learned that the only way to be happy and to make their father happy was by diligent and earnest attention to all duties.[27] When it was evident that Rooney was not applying himself at Harvard, Lee wrote Mary in the tone of a commanding officer, insisting, "It is time for him to begin to think of something else besides running about amusing himself and I wish for him to do so at once." But then, as though to soften his curtness, he went on to explain that the successful attainment of an education depended upon the effort which was put into it. "We have to pay for all we get in this world whether knowledge or pleasure," he said, "and if we get the value of our labor it is all we can ask."[28]

Custis, as the oldest son, was something of a confidant, and, naturally, the chief recipient of Lee's parental instructions. In an early letter Lee related the story of an elderly Connecticut legislator who, when an unusual darkness covered the land and the world was thought to be coming to an end, refused to let the legislature adjourn. "Let candles be brought and the meeting proceed," he insisted, for if the last day was indeed at hand he preferred to be found doing his duty. According to General Long who preserved the story, this was the letter in which Lee was supposed to have said, "Duty . . . is the sublimest word in our language," and to have concluded with the admonition. "Do your duty in all things . . . you cannot do more . . . you should never wish to do less."[29]

Obedience to obligation cost Lee his home, his peace, his dreams, and to no small degree, his life. That to his way of thinking was to be expected. His knowledge of God and his conviction that he was first and foremost the servant of God intensified his sense of responsibility. Regardless of cost, his purpose was to advance what was good, and honorable. Thus, a few days before his surrender he told General Pendleton: "I have never believed we could win against the gigantic combination for our subjection . . . . We had . . . sacred principles to maintain and rights to defend, for which we were duty bound to do our best, even if we perished in the endeavor."[30]

He could be impatient in discharging his duty as he saw it. Refusing to countenance the delays of a clumsy Confederate Congress in supplying the army, he appealed directly to farmer and industrialist alike and bombarded the secretary of war, the chief of ordnance, the quartermaster general, the president, and every other person who might speed deliveries.

When General Joe Johnston vehemently refused to dispatch additional troops to General John B. Magruder for the defense of the Virginia peninsula, Lee began a search for unattached and unarmed men and sent them to Magruder, hoping arms could be supplied from the ranks of the sick and wounded. Even President Davis, who had a compulsion to play the role of commander in chief to the hilt, was handled with something akin to "the wisdom of the serpent and the gentleness of the dove."[31]

By all these means Lee faced misfortune with an astonishing composure. From the ashes of defeat he steadied his friend, General George Jones, saying, "We failed . . . but in the providence of God apparent failure often proves a blessing."[32] As he had done with President Davis, he reminded Charlotte, "all things work together for good if we give Him (God) our love."[33] Mary was told, "I believe in a kind God who has ordered all things for our good."[34] And no doubt he challenged himself many times with Paul's familiar words, "Who shall separate us from the love of Christ? Shall tribulation, or distress, or nakedness, or peril, or sword?"[35] His answer always lay in the Christian confidence, patience and persistence which made it possible for him to assume the offensive and become "more than a conqueror" in the worst of times.

*****

Again, the similarities in Christian faith and practice in Lee and Lincoln are worthy of note. Lincoln had little of Lee's gentle grace. Lee possessed little of Lincoln's art of expression. They hailed from totally different backgrounds with respect to family, education and profession. But if their mutual trust in a living God and similar theological beliefs produced different actions, they also produced an almost identical attitude towards life's burning issues. On October 16, 1857, at Peoria, Illinois, Lincoln said: "I am not bound to win, but I am bound to be true, I am not bound to succeed, but I am bound to live by the light I have."[36] No two sentences could better describe the essence of Robert E. Lee.

CHAPTER NINE

These Are My Principles

When Lee received orders at Fort Mason, Texas, in 1861 to report to General Scott concerning appointment as commander of a new Union army, the state of Texas had already seceded. Lee was shocked nevertheless to learn in San Antonio that a commission of secessionists under the leadership of Benjamin McCullough had already confiscated all military property in the area including Lee's own personal belongings. Indignantly, he turned to his friend, Charles Anderson[1] and requested protection of his equipment until it could be forwarded safely. Explaining that duty and honor forbad submission to the commission and that he would remain with the Union unless Virginia seceded, he concluded, "These are my principles and I must follow them."[2]

Lee's principles were marching orders which sprang from his theological convictions. Ironically, he began with the same premise that his adversary, Abraham Lincoln, did: "As God gives us to see the right."[3] From that base he molded the standards to which he conformed his behavior and developed his principles regarding politics, slavery, and war.

Lee did not presume to think that his principles were always perfect representations of God's will or that they could be counted on to guide him in making right judgments. The question of who was right and who was wrong when two sides began with the same trust in God's guidance, yet reached opposite conclusions, was as perplexing to him as it was to Lincoln, who said, "In the present civil war it is quite possible that God's purpose is something different from the purpose of either party. . . ."[4]

*****

However, no one in Lee's day doubted that the primary objective of government was to provide its people with "life, liberty, and the pursuit of

happiness." This "American Dream" had been born from a renewed interest in such ancient concepts as St. Augustine's City of God and in various
enlightened political philosophies of eighteenth-century culture. Combined,
the sacred and the secular resurrected the ancient belief that man was made
in the image of God and had the God-given right to be free from domination.[5] By the early nineteenth century with this Dream accepted as political
fact, young America eagerly raced toward this noble goal.

Until the question of secession arose, Lee possessed only a casual interest in government per se. As with theology, he was more inclined to
"feel" than to define. It was enough to believe what he had inherited from
his parents' generation, namely that a free government could only be
founded and maintained by the consent of the governed. He added, though,
an important condition. Government must be morally worthy.

As usual, he had spiritual support. The *Catechism*, for example, taught
him that it was a Christian's duty "to honor and obey the civil authority
and meet their just demands."[6] *The Articles of Religion* as established by his
church in 1801 set down "respectful obedience to Civil Authority regularly
and legitimately constituted" as a duty.[7] Paul also taught that "The powers
that be are ordained of God."[8]

Lee was very familiar with these teachings. In each case moral worthi-
ness is demanded or inferred before obedience could be expected. He understood that obedience to law and order was a simple matter as long as they
were not subject to legal and moral tests, but once they were, obedience or
disobedience became complicated. How complicated we have already seen
in Lee's political and moral decision to draw his sword for Virginia.

There were other principles which were similar to Lincoln's description of a "New nation, conceived in liberty, and dedicated to the proposition that all men are created equal," and to his prayer for the "government
of the people, by the people, for the people." Although Lee may not have
used those phrases, he believed in the precepts nevertheless.

While camping along the road to Gettysburg one day, a lady came to
him to say that the residents of the little community were facing hunger
because all the mills were in Confederate hands and she had come to ask
Lee for a distribution of flour. In the course of this conversation she was so
impressed by his gentle manner that on a sudden impulse she asked for his
autograph. "Do you want the autograph of a rebel?" he teased. "General
Lee," she replied boldly, "I am a true Union woman, and yet I ask for bread
and your autograph." Becoming serious Lee replied, "It is to your interest
to be for the Union and I hope you will be as firm in your principles as I am
in mine."[9] Always, he supported such "inalienable rights" — even those of
his foe.

Nor was he any less an advocate of "justice for all." Part of his early
reputation as an officer was gained from his concern to protect potential
victims of injustice. A humorous incident occurred during his Texas days

when a private soldier was brought before him for a preliminary hearing prior to court-martial. Noting the prisoner's nervousness, Lee told him not to worry for he would receive justice, but knowing him, the accused had no doubt of it and replied ruefully, "That is what I am afraid of, sir!"[10]

Probably Lee did not smile at the quip for the relation of justice to liberty was too serious a matter to him. As he understood very well, total liberty is only possible in a vacuum. Whenever one other person is present, liberty is curtailed by that much, and justice becomes operative. Striking the proper balance between them is the perennial problem of a democratic government. When is a law or a deed just and when is it an infringement upon liberty? That is the question.

A third principle included as a human right concerned personal property. When it became evident that some Virginians whose property had been destroyed were planning revenge during their invasion of Pennsylvania, Lee issued General Order No. 71, commanding his men "to abstain with scrupulous care from unnecessary or wanton injury to private property." He also reminded that "the duties enacted upon us by civilization are no less obligatory in the country of the enemy as in our own."[11] This came from the man who had lost Arlington by confiscation and his home by fire.

Human rights were the salient point of the American Dream for Lee, and politics was the means by which a government effectively attained and upheld them. At times his own politics reflected the influence of his father's affiliation with the Federalist Party. Later, he became tacitly identified with the Whigs because it was the party of Southern planters. Finally, after Appomattox, he became a Democrat and remained so until his death. Yet until the crisis of secession forced a specific choice, politics and political parties were not as important to him as the freedoms and simple justice that they were designed to protect.

It must be remembered that in 1861 Colonial tradition with its belief in separate state governments, particularly in the agrarian South, had not lost its significance. Lee's parents and the parents of most of his peers had been citizens of one of the Thirteen Colonies. At the same time they had pledged their lives, fortunes, and sacred honor to their new nation. Few of these believed, though, that that same nation had the authority to override the rights of individual states.

Slavery, as we shall see, was a central issue for many in the war, but the North also fought for the preservation of the Union and the South for the rights of the individual states. Neither side could be persuaded that it had any other recourse. Both sides believed that in honor they could do no less. And the result? An estimated 325,000 Americans were killed in battle; 500,000 more were seriously wounded; 56,000 died in prison; and an incredible 284,000 died of disease.[12] Even if the figures are not exact half their numbers would speak as forcibly of the tragic consequences when contending principles go to war.

Despite his political convictions, Lee made a point of dodging political entanglements. This was true for him as a peacetime officer and also during the war. Even after Appomattox he remained resolute in his decision never to stand for any political office although it was obvious that he could have had any post he desired in the South and even some in the North. There was, however, one exception. He did join with some Northern, as well as Southern leaders in opposing U. S. Grant, the Republican candidate for president.

In politics as in every other facet of his being, Lee reached his principles by way of a rational faith in God. While he did not place politics in the same category as the evils of war and the shame of slavery, he was no less inclined to turn to Divine Providence for guidance and beseech public officials and private citizens to do the same. If in order to obtain elements which comprise "the good life," it was necessary for people to "render unto Caesar the things which are Caesar's," let them do so, he believed, but let Caesar also remember to render "unto God the things which are God's."[13] Together private citizens and public officers must trust their Creator, seek His will, obey His moral laws, and work patiently to carry out His purpose. These were Lee's principles, and he lived by them.

*****

Contrary to what one would expect in view of his chosen profession, he was a total disbeliever in the divine right to wage war. He looked upon war as a breakdown of politics, the consequences of which were "horrid enough at best, surrounded by all the amelioration of civilization and Christianity."[14] It existed solely because the world in its sinfulness had not learned to govern itself with understanding, forgiveness and love.

Possibly he had never heard of Augustine's theory of "a just war" which was conceived after the sacking of Rome by the Visigoths; nor of the position taken later by some theologians who also stated that "[n]ot all wars are equally just and not all contestants are equally right."[15] However, whether knowledgeable of these beliefs or not, Lee believed in "just war." He believed that the choice offered in 1861 was either abject surrender to aggression or a meeting of an immoral force with a moral one. He wrote the secretary of war about saving "the honor of all families from pollution" and "our social system from destruction."[16] Two years later in a General Order to troops he wrote that they should fight for "the freedom of his country, the honor of his people, and the security of his home."[17] There was little doubt in his mind that as evil as war was, it was justified when the virtue of the cause outweighed the alternative means of protecting it.

Such a view has been called "The Compromise Ethic." Both in his attitude toward slavery and in post-war reconciliation this view was a concession to circumstances which he (and Lincoln) made more than once. Many sincere Christians were of similar mind during the Second World

War, holding to the belief that democracy with all its weaknesses was still closer to God's will than Naziism.

Perhaps Lee regretted the necessity of choosing between a relative and an absolute principle. His enjoyment of army life at West Point and during his early years in the service was in marked contrast to the attitude he developed later. While his experience in Mexico left him in no doubt of war's unqualified evil, the camaraderie of the peacetime army was a source of real satisfaction. Prior to 1861, commissioned officers in the regular army numbered little more than a thousand men and almost constituted a private club. If they did not know their fellow officers personally, they at least knew them by reputation. Thus, in 1859 Lee could write, "You have heard me say that cordiality and friendship in the army was the greatest attraction to the service. It is that, I believe, which has kept me in it so long, and it is that which makes me fear to leave it."[18] Fellowship was as important to Lee's military life as it was to his spiritual one.

On the other hand he could not condone the ultimate purpose for which the army existed. When his daughter, Mildred, consulted him regarding a school paper that she had been assigned to write about the farmer, the soldier, and the sailor, he stated without equivocation that "The first is the most useful citizen, the last two necessary evils which will disappear when the world becomes sufficiently Christianized."[19]

When Markie Williams inquired about a military career for her brother, Orton, with similar candor he replied, "I can advise no young man to enter the Army. The same application, the same self-denial, the same endurance in any other profession will advance him faster and further. Nothing but an unconquerable passion for military life would induce me to recommend the military profession."[20]

These two letters were written before Fort Sumter, and he had yet to learn that nothing was as bitter as war itself. The Mexican campaign provided only a weak foretaste of the carnage that resulted from the bloody conflict between the North and South which proved to be everything Lee feared it might be and more. It provided the last of the old-fashioned battles when men paused to dress their ranks in open fields during an attack to the encouraging beat of drums and was the first where Americans waged total war against isolated farms and defenseless cities. Navy ironclads reduced wooden gun boats to impotent anachronisms over night. For the first time railroads moved troops to battle with unheard of speed, while the telegraph sped communications with lightning velocity.[21] Spencer carbine rifles replaced smoothbore muskets and multiplied firepower sevenfold. Canons were mounted on railroad flatcars, foretelling the "Big Berthas" of the First World War. The six-barrel Gatling gun was patented, and telescopic sights for rifles were introduced. Water torpedoes and land mines became commonplace while the Confederate *Hunley*, the first submarine to be used effectively, sank the USS *Housatonic* in Charleston Harbor.

The techniques and weapons of war were developed in a hundred ways, but the medical practices and hospital treatment continued with the unconscionable brutality of the Dark Ages. Following Second Manasses, the Union wounded were moved to Fairfax, Virginia, in springless wagons along rutted roads which stretched for miles. There was little or no water, and on arrival no hospital, no medicine, no food, and only a handful of doctors. Some hay was thrown carelessly over the side of a slope where the seriously wounded were placed out in the open to await the ministrations of the surgeons and a small number of volunteers who cared enough to help — one of them, Clara Barton.

Conditions were even worse following the Battle of Chancellorsville. As the Union army retreated north, long lines of wagons were sent bumping over dusty roads to Fredericksburg where the few remaining citizens of that devastated city, with neither supplies nor experience, came forward to nurse their enemies. Gettysburg, a farming community of two thousand inhabitants, was inundated by some twenty-two thousand wounded men, and Lee's line of hospital wagons was reported to have stretched seventeen miles. During the war some 284,000 blue- and gray-clad soldiers died of disease.[22] Needless to say, the suffering was greater in the South because of a lack of medicine and anesthetics. As for the maimed of mind, they received no treatment at all.

This was the kind of full-scale conflict with its employment of vast numbers of inexperienced young civilians and the immeasurable pain and misery they were forced to endure which increased Lee's abhorrence of war. He was human enough to be moved by success and his first reaction during the Battle of Fredericksburg was one of elation as he watched blue-clad men running in confusion to the accompaniment of Rebel yells. However, his joy was quickly transformed into overwhelming sadness by the sight of so many lifeless bodies and the cries of unattended wounded. Turning apologetically to General Longstreet he confessed, "It is well that war is so terrible — we should grow too fond of it."[23]

An interesting mark of Lee's growing sensitivity can be found by comparing his detailed description to his family of the artillery duel at Vera Cruz with his later refusal to offer the slightest descriptive hint of battle horrors.

B. H. Hill, who surmised that Lee would be Jefferson Davis's successor in office, also described him as "Caesar without his crimes, Bonaparte without his ambition, and George Washington without his crown of success."[24] The words are a fitting tribute but their martial spirit does not do justice to the moral courage which could confess the sin of war yet choose it as a means of fulfilling what he conceived to be a higher duty and a more exacting obedience. Again, the children's hymn describing modern sainthood can apply when it says, "And one was a soldier."[25]

*****

As with their principles regarding war, both Lee and Lincoln adopted a "compromise ethic" respecting slavery which fell short of their private convictions. Both, as Lincoln said of himself, were "controlled by events" that they could not override,[26] and both were forced to compromise as the only feasible way of attaining their primary goals.

Lincoln compromised because saving the Union came first and to add his voice to the abolitionists' course on slavery was to risk much needed support. Lee did so because he had to man and equip an army for defenses against invasion, and to insist upon an anti-slavery principle at this point was to destroy that priority. Both men saw their half measures as another name for "Reason", but neither ceased to pray for a better solution.

Lee and a great majority of Southerners, including those who possessed no slaves, expressed a post-war happiness that slavery had been abolished.[27] When offered command of the Union army, he could only say in frustration, "If I owned the four million slaves I would cheerfully sacrifice them to preserve the Union."[28] In 1859 he wrote ruefully to Custis that his father-in-law had left him "an unpleasant legacy in making him responsible for the Arlington slaves."[29] In 1860 he recorded his distaste of efforts to renew the slave trade saying, "I am opposed to it on every ground."[30] (With Mary he joined and contributed to the American Colonization Society which had been founded in 1817 to purchase land on the western part of the continent so that Christian black people who desired to do so could return to the home of their forefathers once they were freed.) One Sunday when attending St. Paul's Church in Richmond and it came time for the members of the congregation to approach the altar for their communion, they were surprised to see a black man also coming forward. While they returned in their pews, Lee rose and came to kneel beside the black man whereupon the congregation did likewise.

It would be untrue, however, to say that Lee had no hint of prejudice. In Texas, having chased his Indian opponents over hill and plain, he saw the bloody results of their attacks on white settlers. He sat with them in their tribal councils and felt an irritation that he did not trouble to conceal. "These people give a world of trouble to man and beast," he wrote, "and poor creatures, they are not worth it."[31]

He was also unconvinced that black labor could be used effectively on plantations. During post-war days he betrayed a surprising bigotry in a letter to a distant cousin, urging him to dismiss the blacks who had remained on his force as free men, for they were irresponsible.[32] A letter to his son, Rob, showed a similar distrust. There is no denying that while his affection reached out to the Uncle Remus type of black man described by Joel Chandler Harris, Lee appears to have doubted the enterprise and dependability of the field hand.

There were five components of Lee's principles regarding slavery, which are antiquated and difficult to comprehend fully when viewed through a contemporary prism. Four of these components were of the "yes, but" category.

First. He denounced the transportation of blacks in chains to America as an inhuman disgrace but took consolation in the thought that God in His mercy would bring them to an ultimate good by converting them to Christianity and, as soon as adequately prepared, to an enlightened citizenship in their new land. Bishop Meade and a number of church leaders agreed. They believed that as God had sent the white man to Jamestown in 1607 not only to trade with the Indians but to convert them, so the black man was brought to these shores not only to provide labor but to learn of Christ. Thus, though they could not condone the inhumanity of slavery, the horror of slave ships, and the brutality of "Simon Legrees," they thought their "temporary evils" would be balanced by an ultimate and eternal good. The knowledge that by 1859 there were approximately 468,000 church members among the South's slave population appeared to illustrate that the goal of Christianity was being attained.[33]

Second. He admitted that to chain human beings to a system which denies any opportunity of development was a sin against God and man. But having done so, to release the slaves *en masse* when he believed that they were unprepared to cope in society was no less criminal. Despite periodic feelings of guilt the problem was more of a rational one for Lee. He could not suffer pangs of sympathy for a race he believed to be "immeasurably better off here than in Africa."[34] He did not deny the immorality of slavery any more than he denied the immorality of war. Nor did he question the right of every slave to be free. The only questions were, "When?" and "How?"

Third. Lee believed that the best solution to the problem lay with the owners. To attain any measure of equality for the enslaved blacks, time was required to train and educate them. Freeing them by force would arouse bitterness in the ones who could do most for their spiritual and secular development. The apprenticeship system appended to England's Act of Emancipation in 1834, making former owners responsible for helping freed slaves adjust to a new life, was surely familiar to him. He must also have known about the disastrous consequences of that impractical law which gave past owners neither incentive nor authority for assisting blacks.[35] It is too much to expect that plantation owners never discussed this act, or that those men like Lee did not find confirmation for their belief that owners should assume responsibility for preparing their untrained people for freedom while they were still owners. No one could better exercise the mild and salutary influence of Christianity than the owners, and no one was more morally obligated to do so.

Fourth. Only a wise and merciful God knew when the injustices committed against black people would be abolished, but a beginning had to be made. Gradual emancipation should become the rule and slaves should be freed as quickly as they were equipped to make their own way. Granted it would be a slow process for "The doctrine and miracles of our Savior required nearly two thousand years to convert but a small part of the human race . . ."[36] Mary Lee possessed the same attitude. Her advice to a young cousin who had inherited slaves from his parents' estate was, "Let no motive of worldly interest induce you to act an unkind or ungenerous part towards them."[37] She also began to teach black children the elements of Christianity at Fort Monroe and complained bitterly when provisions were not made for blacks to worship along with whites at church services.

Finally, the North's military victory erased all of Lee's carefully reasoned arguments overnight. The abolition of slavery for which he had hoped and prayed became a reality although not in the manner he would have chosen. Despite the excesses of the Reconstruction era, uncontrolled emancipation proved not to be as disastrous as he had anticipated and in fact was far more desirable than the structured and gradual freedom for which he had contended. So as always, he turned to his "God knows what is best" faith and accepted the defeat of his views with the same equanimity that he had accepted the defeat of his army. At least he could now put aside his "Compromise Ethic" and rejoice that the institution of slavery was finally at an end.

The only option for Lee was to apply as many elements of Christian love which could offer dignity, trust, affection, and proof that he was not color blind in respect to race. In fact, he did all he could to cooperate with what he conceived to be God's will for the black people in his time and place. It was the best he could do *under the circumstances.*

*****

As noted, Lee's principles, whether respecting politics, war or slavery, grew out of his understanding of the Doctrine of Man: man's values in the sight of God and his rights in the Brotherhood of Man. In every age, however, there are questions of blurred complexity which force individuals to take the approach Lee did. Indeed, his example can serve as a model for Christian procedure: (1) to pray earnestly for guidance; (2) to adopt principles consistent with what the Will of God is conceived to be; and (3) to leave one's honest actions to the judgment of Heaven.

CHAPTER TEN

To Heal Our Country's Wounds

When the defeated Confederate general made his journey to Lexington in September of 1865, he must have known his new life would provide neither a peaceful sanctuary nor a leisurely opportunity for academic pursuits. Peace was declared, but it was only a paper peace and a disheartened South turned once more to its former military leader like a frightened child to its father. Letters came pouring in from California, Iowa, Indiana, and the Montana Territory, as well as from distant countries such as Mexico and Brazil. What was wanted was guidance and inspiration in the search for sanity, and no one had forgotten either Lee's show of faith and affection or his devotion to duty and discipline.

The struggle to bring his people back into the Union was his final battle and finest victory. He possessed no organized army of supporters, no cunningly devised political strategy, and no subtle pressure tactics designed to trick former forces into offering a warm welcome. He was only one man, a seemingly defenseless David facing a legion of Goliaths, but like David he was armed with an inner strength. Supported by his trust in God and faith in man, he exemplified a statesmanship which mollified his antagonists, reassured his followers, and to no small degree established a climate for permanent peace throughout the land.

History has described him during the last five years of his life as a "conciliator," but the title lacks breadth. St. Paul wrote that "Christ . . . had broken down the middle wall of partition between us,"[1] and added that God ". . . hath given to us a ministry of reconciliation."[2] The two passages speak to divine initiative and human response. Christian reconciliation originates with the down thrust of God's love for humanity and climaxes with the outreach of a person's love for family. It was this outreach that Lee undertook. There was no appeasement, no blind acceptance of injustice, and no sacrifice of principle. Instead there was a spiritual thrust of faith and love against "the middle wall of partition: with a persistent pressure of Christian ethics. Together, they gradually wore away the former enemy's resistance to reunion.

*****

The victorious Ulysses S. Grant, following the retreat of the famished, tattered Confederate army from Petersburg to Appomattox, prophesied that, "The suffering which must exist in the South next year will be beyond calculation."[3] His prediction was fulfilled to the letter; economically, politically, and emotionally. Vacant stores, boarded and padlocked, in virtually every community testified to the economic collapse of the population. Trade was paralyzed because no United States currency was available and no credit extended. The scarred and lifeless land was dotted with charred skeletons of a former way of life, and only an occasional stark chimney stood as a monument to defeat. At least 260,000 men in butternut rags lay in their graves. No exact reckoning of the disabled and deranged was made, or could be. A reported 4,000,000 slaves had been told they were free, but most were ill equipped by lack of education and the absence of resources for their change of status. Former masters and former slaves joined with marauders and the dispossessed to roam the naked earth. Towns and villages were crowded with homesick occupation troops, avaricious carpetbaggers, scalawags,[4] and in too many instances corrupt officials. Elected representatives were denied their seats in Congress and sent home. Southern states remained severed from the Union, disenfranchised, and under siege by the relentless "Reconstruction" members of the United States Congress.

To such grim conditions a bewildered people responded with futility, despair, and hostility. Many young battle-scarred veterans turned to the bottle. Their numbers grew so rapidly that the *Alexandria Gazette* had to admit the "vice of intemperance is alarmingly on the increase," while the *Richmond Sentinel* was more blunt in stating that "Thousands of our must gifted and promising young men are fast becoming confirmed sots."[5]

Countless Southerners also found doubts about their faith. The Cause had been considered sacred and one which a just God was certain to support for Providence always defended the right. Yet, in spite of the assurances of clergymen, President Davis, newsmen, and General Lee himself, the Cause was lost. What had become of the help from God? It was a question which could not be answered with either spiritual or temporal satisfaction and a wavering faith contributed to much despondency.

The South had reason to expect better. After the war with Mexico, the victorious United States had been lenient. When peace negotiations began in 1848, Lee wrote Mary that "For myself, I would not exact more now than I would have taken before the commencement of hostilities, as I should wish nothing but what is just." In the same letter he explained, ". . . we have the right by the laws of war, of dictating the terms of peace . . . but I would be generous in exercising it."[6] Such thoughts were representative of the nation's merciful attitude toward the vanquished foe.

Abraham Lincoln in his second inaugural address had followed a similar line, and the South remembered the goodwill embodied in the words: "With malice toward none; with charity for all . . . let us strive or to finish the work we are in; to bind up the nation's wounds; . . . to do all which may achieve and cherish a just and lasting peace among ourselves, and with all nations."[7] President Andrew Johnson also issued a proclamation on May 29, 1866, stating that "clemency will be liberally extended as may be consistent with the facts of the case and the peace and dignity of the United States."[8]

General Grant had shown similar magnanimity that Palm Sunday in the McLean House at Appomattox, and Lee was grateful for the consideration given his troops, admitting that the generous terms being offered at his surrender would "do much toward the reconciliation of our people.[9] Then, as the Southern commander mounted Traveler to ride away from the unhappy scene, the Union general and his staff in a further gesture of respect and goodwill followed him onto the porch and removed their hats. Never before or since has a commanding general of the United States Army shown such admiration for an adversary. He also ordered his men to refrain from cheering or firing volleys in celebration of the victory. "The war is over," he said. "The rebels are again our countrymen, and the best way of showing our rejoicing will be to abstain from all such demonstration.[10]

His troops did as bidden. One of the most touching aspects of the surrender was described by a Union officer who told how the Northern soldiers came to "Carry Arms"—the marching salute as the proud, used-up, Confederate ranks marched by in a column to stack arms. On seeing this General Gordon commanded his ragged men to salute in similar fashion. "On our part," the Union officer said, "not a sound of trumpet more, nor roll of drum; not a cheer, nor word nor whisper of vain-glorying, but an awed stillness rather, and breath-holding, as if it were the passing of the dead."[11] So it was that the Army of Northern Virginia passed into history.

Manifestly, at that point leniency characterized the North's attitude. But Lee had not yet heard the cry of the avenger. The parents and families of 360,000 dead in the North clamored for reprisal. The unsatisfied abolitionists shouted for more revenge. The ambitious Northern politicians heard them, counted their votes, and acted accordingly.

But first, on Good Friday, the man who had asked the Union army bands to play "Dixie," counseled "Let 'em up easy," and reproached the unforgiving nature of avengers with the warning, "Judge not that ye be not judged,"[12] was shot to death at Ford's Theater by John Wilkes Booth. From that moment uncompromising congressmen, under the leadership of Thaddaeus Stevens of Pennsylvania, took control of Congress. Jefferson Davis was imprisoned at Fort Monroe and, unbelievably, Congressman

George W. Julian of Indiana called for his execution "in the name of God." Senator Charles Sumner, the abolitionist leader from Massachusetts, thundered that the South had committed suicide by its rebellion and should be considered dead as far as any equality with the North was concerned. And newsman William Lloyd Garrison demanded total domination by the victors, insisting that the powers of Hell were still strong and defiant in the South and only awaited an opportunity to work their evil. In their spirit of revenge they called their program "Peace," but the South called it another form of slavery.

Before Lee had settled down at his Franklin Street residence in Richmond, word was brought that he had been found guilty of treason by a Federal Grand Jury in Norfolk. Try as he might, the new president in Washington was unable to stem such acts and a Joint Committee on Reconstruction was created by Congress with Stevens as its chairman. Subcommittees were also named to examine conditions regionally, and Senator Jacob M. Howard of Michigan was appointed to head the one which was to pass judgment on Virginia and the Carolinas.

Ostensibly, one purpose of these committees was to examine the temper of the Southern states and offer recommendations regarding their right to representation in the Houses of Congress. However, those under examination likened them to inquisitors who proceeded too enthusiastically without regard for courtesy or compassion. Predictably, the insensitive actions of these committees created reactions throughout the South. These reactions multiplied Lee's difficulties a hundred fold in his effort to tear down "the middle wall of partition."

He received notice to appear before Senator Howard's subcommittee in Washington on February 17, 1886, only a few months after his arrival in Lexington. Apparently, the summons was motivated as much by curiosity as enmity, and if the proceedings were bluntly formal, they were not disrespectful. A two-hour examination focused on the enfranchisement of the black man; alleged cruelty to Union prisoners of war; the contingency of Southern support of a foreign power in event of war against the United States; and the unwillingness of the South to condemn Jefferson Davis as a war criminal. The questions might have provoked incriminating answers from a less disciplined man, but Lee avoided the obvious traps with dignified ease.

There were personal questions as well. Had he taken an oath of allegiance to the Confederate government? Was he not in fact misled by traitorous politicians into casting his lot with the secessionists? When Lee had an opinion based upon first-hand knowledge, he did not hesitate to express it. He did not believe he had taken an oath of allegiance to the Confederate government, although he might have done so when he received his army commission. No, he had not been misled into drawing his sword against the North by outside influences. The decision was his alone. And,

President Davis could in no way be considered a traitor for obeying the will of the several states, all of which considered themselves free and able to make independent decisions. He proved to be an adroit witness who was humble but not obsequious, restrained but not defensive, and Senator Howard's subcommittee finally excused him from further testimony.

As the news was released regarding his new post at Washington College, a negative reaction resounded throughout the North. The *New York Independent* wrote, "the bloodiest and guiltiest traitor in all the South, that man we make the President of a college."[13] Mountains of mail arrived at the White House, most of it like the one which asked, "Aren't you ashamed to give Lee the privilege of being President of a college? Satan wouldn't have him open the door for fresh arrivals."[14]

At the same time Southern "scalawags" who had held their peace for four years began to rise up and join the North in a discordant chorus against Lee. They charged that he had approved the formation of clandestine organizations and had become an "invisible member" of the Ku Klux Klan, which had been organized in 1866.

No evidence was ever produced to validate this claim. Not even the records of the Klan claimed his membership or any other type of moral or financial support. Besides, early members of the Klan insisted that their organization was created originally as a "hilarious social club." In spite of riots in some cities which were little more than organized massacres of blacks, the Klan claimed that during its early years it was "no more than a practical joke."[15] With such a reputation, it is inconceivable that Lee would have been interested in membership. Moreover, the Klan's character would have been too repugnant to his nature and to the role he had chosen to play in the post-war years.[16]

During this period the anger of not a few Southerners was beginning to erupt. Fear, hunger and harsh treatment by the victors were arousing their instinct for self-preservation and providing reason for retaliation. Secret societies, and some not so secret, did come into existence. Young men, especially many too young to have served in the army, grew increasingly aggressive. More and more of the large silent majority began to nurse a smoldering hatred towards the North which in some ways exceeded anything that was felt during the military conflict. In Lee's adopted community, the *Lexington Gazette* called the Joint-Report of the Committee on Reconstruction a "devilish iniquity and malignant wickedness" which no Southerner could read "without invoking the righteous indignation of heaven."[17] Even so mild a man as Bishop Beverly Tucker of Virginia penned a poem, one stanza of which reads:

> Though the battle may be over
> Yet its horrors still remain;
>
> Though the cannon's voice is silent
> Still we hear the clanking chain.[18]

While many of the North were denouncing Lee as a rebel who deserved trial and punishment, most of the South continued to hail him as "the realized King Arthur."[19] There were, however, a significant number of diehards who fiercely resented his cooperative attitude towards former foes, believing it indicated a public confession of guilt and repentance. Even his move to Washington College was interpreted as an effort to divorce himself from further involvement in his people's plight. Thus, like every mediator, he became the target for both extremes, neither of which could recognize, or believe, his application of Christian love.

Some ex-Confederates condemned his efforts for reconciliation as a treacherous betrayal of friends by an overly anxious appeasement of enemies. Others who had hailed him as a savior when he applied his belief in law and order to Southern rights, turned on him with venomous hostility once he applied the same principles to Northern rights. Such accusations added to his difficulty as a reconciler and cut deep into his soul.

It is impossible to estimate the result of so much hatred. There were New York crowds which shouted "Hang Lee! Hang Lee!"[20] and individuals like the Indiana congressman who shouted his outrage over the fact that Lee remained out of jail, when he should have been executed. Many former abolitionists now worked to prevent any moral or financial support of his college.

Predictably, his disciplined character accepted such malice without a public rebuttal, but at least some of its effect is revealed in a letter to Markie Williams. He explained that he was being labeled such a monster that he hesitated to visit loved ones for fear of bringing misfortune upon them. Then, no doubt with a touch of depression, he exclaimed, "My cause is dead! I am homeless — I have nothing on earth."[21] He also confessed being driven from a sleepless bed at night by thoughts of all the suffering in the South.

Such reactions indicate something of the inner turmoil occasioned by Northern hatred. To whom could he turn for advice? Where could he find salve for his wounds? How could the doubts about himself be laid to rest? There was only his faith — and it proved to be enough. With it he held tight to the conviction that a just God would right everything in the end, and he picked his way resolutely through the maze of fear and hatred in the exercise of his special ministry.

The best and practically the only defense offered was in a letter to General P. T. E. Beauregard in which he reminded him that patriotism sometimes required a different action at one period than at another even though the desire to do what was right was unchanged. He pointed to General Washington, explaining how he fought for the British against the French under General Braddock but in a few years fought against the British with the French as changing circumstances often called for changes in policy. It was the same under the circumstances, and being controlled by events[22] that had moved him and Lincoln in the past. Meanwhile, his reply to Southern critics remained gentle, forgiving, and understanding.

*****

There were three main objectives in the healing of his country's wounds. The first was to identify himself with his people, to suffer what they suffered, and to call upon all fugitives to do likewise. The flood of invitations from former companions-in-arms living all over the world did not cease, but he made his position quite clear when Matthew Fontaine Maury, the one-time United States oceanographer and experimenter with Confederate underwater torpedoes, invited him to escape to Mexico two months after the surrender. "The thought of abandoning the country and all that must be left in it is abhorrent to my feelings," he replied, "and I prefer to struggle for its restoration and share its fate, rather than to give up all as lost . . ."[23] The answer was the same when General Beauregard inquired about his plans for the future. Though overwhelmed by the unexpected offer of a luxurious mansion and estate in England, and another insurance corporation's invitation with large stipend, this time in the company of friends, he still could not be persuaded to leave the Old Dominion. Deep inside was a sturdy determination to assist in her recovery.

His family understood and approved the role he had assumed. Characteristically, Mary, "The Unreconstructed Rebel," continued to write intemperately to close personal friends. "It is bad enough to be victims of tyranny," she complained, "but when it is wielded by such cowards and base men as Butler [and] Thaddaeus Stevens . . . it is indeed intolerable. The Country that allows such scum to rule them," she continued, "must fast be going to destruction . . . My indignation cannot be controlled. . . ."[24] She did control it, however, and was careful to see that such private opinions gave place to conformity with her husband's desire "to accomplish something for the good of mankind and the glory of God."[25]

Although the three girls found adjustment somewhat difficult in Lexington and had few friends there, they also kept any negative thoughts to themselves. Neither did they appear to resent their father's refusal of the $10,000 annual salary proposed by the Knickerbocker Life Insurance Company, nor the opportunity for years of comfort in England. His point of view was accepted willingly, and they attempted to live as benefitted the times, contenting themselves with occasional visits to friends and relatives.

Even so, Lee was not hesitant in reminding them of their responsibilities to their "native land." He cautioned Mildred when she was in Baltimore on plainness and simplicity of dress, early hours, rational amusements. Lee asked her to bear in mind "that it will not be becoming to a Virginia girl now to be fine or fashionable." Gentility and self-respect required moderation he added, and it was important for her to practice self-denial while so many of her people were suffering.[26]

He was justly proud of the examples his sons were setting. Custis had joined the faculty of nearby Virginia Military Institute; Rooney had returned to farming at White House Plantation, and Rob had begun to till the soil at Romancocke. Still, he was never adverse to reminding Rooney not to spend money freely, saying, "We have all, now, to confine ourselves strictly to necessities . . . Every one must look to his material interests now, as labor is our only resource."[27]

Twenty-two-year-old Rob's frugality, on the other hand, caused some dismay and a reversal of such conservatism. His youngest son was living contentedly as a bachelor in a sagging roofed overseer's cabin of ancient vintage, and exhibiting no concern for a lack of silver, china, and the cheapest furnishings. Lee said little as he inspected the premises beyond suggesting the investment of a small sum for these necessities; but on his return to Richmond he sent Rob a set of plated forks and spoons and began to intensify his search for a suitable wife for his youngest son.

He did not hesitate, however, to recommend a stand-still course for everyone. The temptation to flee for fear of reprisal, or in hope of better opportunity, was strong. Migration to a new life in a new land seemed the only logical way to many veterans. Emperor Maximillian of Mexico was making it easy with an open-door policy. But Lee maintained it was incumbent upon good soldiers to remain at home, become good citizens, and risk the future along with their countrymen.

The second major objective of his ministry of reconciliation was to exemplify an unconditional dedication to law and order. Although believing he and his men were protected from Federal prosecution by the terms of his surrender and the paroles given at that time[28] he was careful to demonstrate a continuing support of constitutional government by conforming to every regulation. While still in Richmond, he wrote General Grant of his willingness to comply with President Johnson's Proclamation of Amnesty and Pardon, providing he was eligible to take it and not liable to trial. In the letter he enclosed an application to the president requesting "the benefits and full restoration of all rights and privileges," and asked Custis to make a copy, remarking as he did so that he wanted to set an example for others.[29] But nothing was ever heard from Washington.

Indeed, Lee was so meticulous in conforming to government requirements that in order to avoid the slightest suggestion of unauthorized flight, he wrote the provost marshal in Richmond of his intention to move from the city and requested passports for himself and Custis should they be necessary. Many explanations have been offered concerning the strange delay in restoring his citizenship. Was it too much of a risk for the politically minded to handle? Was it judged illegal because the notary public had not taken the oath himself and was, therefore, ineligible to give it? Was it purposely hidden away? The most recent explanation reported by Charles B. Flood, is the most likely.[30]

Lee followed protocol precisely in mailing his documents to the secretary of state, William H. Seward, but for some reason Seward thought
they had already been recorded and gave them to a friend as a souvenir.
The friend put them away in his desk and forgot about them. One hundred
and five years later they were found in a bundle of papers in the National
Archives.

When Lee did not hear from Washington, he quite naturally assumed
the delay was intentional and made no further effort to be cleared. He had
hoped to prove his own loyalty and at the same time influence others to
prove theirs. He had also wanted to assist any who like Jefferson Davis were
not protected by parole. However, fate ruled otherwise, or was it Providence?

Lee's own obedience remained unencumbered by rationalization or
doubt and was especially evident at Washington College. But whether on
campus, in town, or throughout the South, keeping the peace by allegiance
to law and order was a basic way he had of showing that the war was over
and that God himself wanted a united nation.

Along with his advice to weary veterans to remain in the South, and
subject themselves to constituted authority, was a third counsel to accept
any honorable employment. As he told Colonel Taylor, all former service
men ought to seek work immediately, and "if they cannot do what they
prefer, do what they can."[31] This suggestion never varied. No special revelation was necessary to know that it would be years before the South could
regain its rightful place on the national scene. Meanwhile, it behooved her
people to prepare for that day by accepting any work no matter how menial. What was wanted was the kind of spirit which could put aside personal likes and dislikes and work in unison to develop local trade, industry,
and agriculture. Both his brother Smith and his cousin Hill Carter were
reminded that the South required such work from everyone and especially
work with "white hands."

His admiration for former soldiers who endeavored to follow such a
plan despite the adversity of the times was unqualified. When he read that
one of them who had lost an arm in battle and a fortune to Union confiscation was at work plowing his field without help but with thanksgiving for
his remaining arm, Lee exclaimed, "What a noble fellow!" On learning of a
young officer who was working as a porter for an employer who had served
under him in the ranks, he said enthusiastically that the young men deserved more credit for this than for anything he did in the army."[32]

He never failed to congratulate and encourage men who were striv-
ing under handicaps to succeed with unaccustomed enterprises. These were
the ones who by laboring were offering the kind of example the South so
sorely needed. When the Reverend J. William Jones was preparing to visit
several Southern states Lee sought him out and asked him to convey a
message to any ex-service men he might meet. "[T]ell them," he said, "I
often think of them, try every day to pray for them, and am always grati-
fied to hear of their prosperity."[33]

*****

It was concern for reconciliation as much as natural modesty which caused Lee to avoid discussions of the war and shun public meetings which in any way were connected with it. He even refused to support, publicly, a much favored fundraising project for the orphaned children of Virginia's war dead. Another proposal, this time to collect funds for a Stonewall Jackson monument met with like response. The idea was right, he said, but the timing was wrong. Although at one point he considered writing a history of his campaigns as a vindication of his gallant men, the desire for reconciliation was a major reason for not doing so. Any project that inflamed emotions might be dangerous to his people, his school, and his ministry for peace. So, as he wrote in reply to an invitation from a Gettysburg Identification meeting, he did not think it wise "to keep open the sores of war."[34]

In keeping with this attitude was his suggestion to a lady who lived just outside Lexington. He was taken to see her one day and believing she had a companion spirit she escorted him to a badly damaged tree in her yard. It carried the scars of Union artillery fire which had torn away the limbs and left huge gashes on its trunk from cannonballs. Turning expectantly for sympathy she was surprised and not a little indignant to have him say, "Cut it down, my dear Madam, and forget it."[35]

Moreover, his conviction regarding non-involvement included running for public office. As prophesied, it was a foregone conclusion that once peace was restored he would be considered for some elected post. Even in a city which had cried for his execution there was a right-about and thought given to this possibility. The *New York Herald* proposed his nomination as the Democratic Party's choice for the presidency and wrote columns on his military career in order to prove how qualified he was to run against General U.S. Grant, the Republican's choice. But Lee had not yet been restored to U.S. citizenship so that ended the matter.[36]

However, in Virginia, in spite of military defeat and personal objection, there was a concerted movement to elect him governor. In fact, the drive became so strong Judge Robert Ould of Richmond was compelled to ask if he would accept the nomination. Politely, Lee stated his preference for private life and pointed out his advancing years. But again, his chief argument was that his name on the ballot, any ballot, would incite Northern hostility and prove prejudicial to the people of the state. He continued to call for influential people to run for government posts throughout the South, especially those who could inspire respect for law and order, but his was a different mission and one which would suffer were he to place himself in the political arena.

The same reasoning applied to every form of publicity. "Controversies of all kinds will, in my opinion, only serve to continue excitement and passion, and will prevent the public mind from acknowledgement and acceptance of the truth."[37] That was the response he made to Mrs. Jefferson

Davis' appeal concerning a scurrilous attack made upon her husband for the alleged mistreatment of captured Union men at Andersonville Prison. Even though Davis could not possibly be held guilty for something so obviously beyond his ability to correct, Lee counseled that silence was the best course and in conclusion explained that this was a resolve he had made concerning all the accusations directed at him.

There was an occasion to practice what he preached two months later as he was urged by a friend to defend himself against still another libelous article accusing him of harsh treatment of his slaves, this time in the *Baltimore American*. "The statement is not true"; he replied, "but I have not thought proper to publish a contradiction . . . believing that those who know me would not credit it, and those who do not would care nothing about it."[38]

When Herbert C. Saunders requested permission to publish an account of their discussion the preceding year on the conduct of the war, Lee objected to any public use of what he had considered a private conversation. Politely but firmly he requested that if written, the article should in no way imply his endorsement.

Meanwhile, the United States Congress, having proposed the Fourteenth Amendment during its 1865 session, proceeded to pass the first Reconstruction Act on March 2, 1867, which divided the South into military districts and reduced its representation in Congress. Technically, these acts were concerned with the way to bring the seceded states back into the Union, but in reality they dealt with the status of black people and produced an unhappy mixture of impractical plans and personal self-interest. On both counts they were uniformly resented throughout the South and posed one of the most difficult challenges to Lee's reconciliation ministry.

The defeated states were presided over by governors who possessed totalitarian powers to make appointments, remove office holders, and perform any function consistent with the new laws. In effect, the states were reduced to the status of vassal territories. Representation in Congress was prohibited, virtually every public official who had served in the Confederacy was disqualified from holding public office, and in some instances plantation owners were disfranchised and freed men were given the political authority. When the election of delegates in the Virginia Constitutional Convention was held in October of 1867, seventy-five Radical members, including twenty-five blacks, were elected and thirty-three Conservatives.[39] Such occurrences were an "abomination of desolation" for many and put them in no mood for reconciliation. The hostile and fearful alike, however, continued to turn hopefully to their former commander. Should they boycott the ballot box, organize passive resistance movements, or docilely accept the few remaining crumbs left to them" Lee had already committed himself to seek change by legal process and in a letter to Judge Ould on March 29, 1867, gave a summary of his opinions.

First. Everyone entitled to vote should do so in order to elect the best qualified men to public office.

Second. All good citizens should work to preserve harmony and prevent the separation of people into competitive political camps.

Third. The interests of blacks and whites were inseparably connected and should be preserved by a willing cooperation from both races.

Fourth. On a more personal level he wrote of his determination to remain uninvolved, saying, "It is extremely unpleasant to me, for reasons I think will occur to you, that my name should unnecessarily be brought before the public, and I do not see any good can come of it. I hope therefore you will not publish my letter, but that you will try and allay the strife that I feel may arise in the state."[40]

*****

Lee's efforts to restore peace in the nation were not inspired by "do-good" impulses of a romantic, but rather by the prudent wisdom of a pragmatic Christian. While the states did not require the compromises he had been forced to make in other instances, they did require the intelligence to recognize hard realities, and the faith to proceed in spite of their inflexible limits. He wrote former Virginia Governor Letchef before arriving in Lexington that, "The questions which for years were in dispute between the States and the General Government . . . having been decided against us, it is the part of wisdom to acquiesce in the result, and of candor to recognize the fact . . . . The interests of the State are the same as those of the United States . . . The duty of its citizens, then, appears to me too plain to admit without doubt."[41]

That soon after Appomattox he was convinced of the course the South should take, and, no doubt, the part he would be forced to play in guiding it along that route. He did not organize. He did not publicize. His character, his conduct, and his love spoke for him, and what the South heard was not only a lesson in practical statesmanship, but a sermon on Christian living. Here again, because of his faith, others were able to retain their own.

And yet the effort employed probably cost him his life. Photographs taken during his last five years show all too clearly the rapid deterioration of his physical resources. "The real causes that slowly but steadily undermined his health and led to his death," according to the doctors, were the cumulative strain of the post-war period, along with his efforts at calmness.[42] A price must always be paid for a sacrificial act including the healing of one's country's wounds.

CHAPTER ELEVEN

Loving Kindness

Lee could never be convinced he was worthy of God's love. He expressed this conviction many times in correspondence and conversation and no one, not even Mary, could persuade him otherwise. But worthy or not he had also to admit that by some undeserved miracle he had received this gift and responded with breathless gratitude to the donor and unqualified love for his fellowman. They included young and old, deserving and undeserving, people he did not know and people he knew very well.

There were two adjuncts to the "undeserved miracle." Following his honest recognition of certain weaknesses he began a schedule of prayer and devotional reading which led to the certainty of God's love. Then in corporate and group worship he became aware of the warmth and power generated by a supportive "communion of Saints" which led him to respond to their overtures. Although it probably never occurred to him to distinguish between them, his loving kindness was both "caught" and "taught." It was caught from an invisible God of Love,[1] and taught by the "love unfeigned"[2] of his family, his wife, his Christian friends, and the untold number of anonymous worshippers who knelt with him Sunday after Sunday in prayer and praise.

Love, however, has many faces. There is a family love of fathers, mothers, sisters, and brothers. The love of husband and wife has a rational and spiritual as well as a physical quality which distinguishes it from lust. Friendship is a form of love that by a special chemistry draws unrelated individuals together through common interests and concerns. But Christian love is different. What St. Paul called "charity" has moral and spiritual qualities which characterize our response to the "Gift-Love" of God.[3] Anyone can feel and express other kinds of love, but only Divine Love can penetrate and inspire the response Paul described in I Corinthians.

*****

90

As son, brother and father, Lee's devotion to family ran the gamut of emotions. To Carter and Lee kin he was a happy extrovert who stood in marked contrast to the reserved person the world knew. Any relation, including the most distant cousin, could count on receiving his instant affection and support. Family was vital to him.

His unusually strong attachment to his mother was not Oedipal, but the natural relationship of a boy who all too soon became the only available minister to her needs. The hours he spent making Ann Lee comfortable and helping time to pass transformed their mother-son relationship into a devotion of peers. Although scarcely in his teens, she accepted him as an adult, shared her thoughts, sought his advice and took honest pleasure in his company. He, in turn, tried to be the grown-up she imagined him to be. Of the same temperament, they found it easy to laugh together, weep together, and talk seriously together. So close did their relationship become that whenever Robert left the room his mother's eyes followed him to the door and remained fixed there waiting impatiently for his return.

When he departed for West Point, Ann was forced to leave her Alexandria home and move across the river to Georgetown where Carter had opened his law office. But her condition worsened until finally it became necessary to take her to Ravenworth, the Fitzhugh home near Fairfax, where she could receive twenty-four hour attention. By the time Robert graduated her condition had become terminal, and he raced to her side to resume his nursing. He mixed her medicines, ran her errands, and sat helplessly by as life drained slowly from her tired body. She died June 10, 1829, when he was twenty-two years of age but not before bequeathing him her knowledge of God and love and human kindness.

When Light Horse Harry Lee, sick of body and soul, departed for his self-imposed exile on the island of Barbados, he was almost as much a myth to Robert as a flesh and blood parent. Robert could, of course, recall evenings by the fireside when his father had entertained the family with fascinating adventure stories. His young mind would never forget the Baltimore horror when his father was beaten by a drunken mob and left for dead. Along with other members of the family, he listened attentively to the sage advice in letters from far away. Yet his father's image depended largely upon his mother's glowing accounts, and to a lesser degree, upon tales told of his exploits by former troopers who resided in the neighborhood. Those descriptions vested his sire with an aura which never totally dissipated.

As Robert became old enough to study Harry Lee's political and military activities he began to form a much clearer picture of his famous father. Out of acquired knowledge and legendary lore grew an increasing respect for Harry's virtues and a somewhat compassionate understanding of his defeat which made Robert both proud and defensive. Whenever he talked of his parent, he was prone to overload his conversation with heroic anecdotes and praise and when he wrote of him he did so in a laudatory manner he would never have used to describe himself. From his mother, Lee inherited his "manly beauty" and temperament. His father gave him his physique and boundless energy. How much influence he exerted is difficult to assess. There can be little doubt that Robert was affected by Harry's moral and ethical preachments and by his political loyalty for his state over his nation.

On an inspection tour of coastal defenses in 1862, he took time with his aide and eventual biographer, A. L. Long, to visit Harry Lee's grave. Making his way to the site on Cumberland Island,[4] he stood with bowed head in prayerful silence before the unpretentious headstone and on his departure quietly plucked a wild flower to carry with him as a memento. Eight years later when he and Agnes made the prescribed journey South, he returned. Again he stood in silent prayer while his daughter decorated the grave with fresh flowers.

Over the years several of Robert's brothers and sisters became scattered beyond hope of reunion. Carter was nearby but almost nine years his senior; too far removed in interests for close childhood ties. The sympathy of Anne's family in Baltimore was with the Union, and her son, Louis, served on the staff of his uncle's most scorned foe, General Pope. However, Lee did not betray the slightest resentment. Smith was not only the closest in age, he was the most compatible. They grew up together, and as far as possible raised their children together.[5] Mildred, meanwhile, was living in Paris as the wife of Edward Vernea Childe and practically out of reach. Of all the children Robert seemed to have inherited the largest share of family loyalty. It was he who initiated most of the correspondence, created occasions for periodic visits, displayed great concern for Anne's failing eyesight, named one of his daughters after Mildred and joined with his oldest brother in editing and reproducing their father's *Memoirs.*

What we have seen of Lee's counseling his children, his concern for their education, anxiety for their safety, and especially his eagerness for their growth in Christian faith and practice mark him as more than an average father. His wisdom in knowing when to speak and when to remain silent, when to punish and when to encourage, when to advise and when to permit independent thought can still serve as an admirable example for any parent. He was a comfortable sort of father who joked and teased and petted his offspring, yet who at the same time made it quite clear that obedience and morality and loyalty to duty were not only wanted but expected.

When Rooney, as a small boy, almost severed the tips of two fingers with a chopping knife his father wrote Custis that his brother "may probably lose his fingers and be marred for life. You cannot conceive what I suffer at the thought."[6] It was the same with Annie who accidentally injured an eye with a pair of scissors and aroused a special tenderness throughout her short life. In his will he expressed the wish that she "may be particularly provided for."[7] Mildred also received special attention. When she contracted typhoid fever she insisted no one could nurse her but her father and so, perhaps with a little pride, he sat by her bed night after night and watched over her with tender patience until "Precious Life," as he called her, recovered.

Young Mary, Custis, and Agnes were different. Mary, the oldest, proved to be an independent spirit, a poor correspondent, and an inveterate traveler who insisted on living her own life in her own way. Custis lacked Rooney's light-heartedness. By nature he was of serious mind which at times made him seem aloof, a condition to which frequent depressions contributed, particularly in later years. Yet he was brilliant of mind and generous to a fault. Agnes, who was to die at thirty-two, only a few years after her father, was rarely in good health. Probably that was the reason strangers considered her reserved and even conceited. But she was an exceptional nurse and her father chose her as a companion for his prolonged journey through the South after the war. Lee could have told each of his children what he one time wrote Mildred, ". . . all appearances to the contrary, you will never receive such love as is felt for you by your father and mother."[8] In return, his youngest son, Rob, called him "an ideal father,"[9] and his sisters and brothers would have said no less.

*****

Mary Custis and Robert were childhood acquaintances who must have accompanied their parents many times on visits between Arlington and Alexandria. As Mary matured, however, it was Robert's brother, Carter, who first expressed admiration for her, and he was not alone. Many young men were beginning to knock at Arlington's door including a flamboyant young Congressman from Tennessee named Sam Houston who would ride over from Washington.

No one would have called Mary a breath-taking beauty, but there was an undeniable appeal in her sparkling personality, smiling eyes, and aristocratic bearing. These were the attributes which first caused his friendship to develop into something deeper. Finally, one day he proposed over a piece of fruitcake in the Arlington dining room and was accepted.

At home with servants to assist in keeping her attractive and the house neat, Mary's shortcomings went unnoticed. But once she set up housekeeping for herself the secret was out. As noted she was apt to be untidy, careless in domestic matters and totally incapable of managing her time. A short while after their marriage her husband found it necessary to warn guests of these facts and explain, "The spirit is willing, but the flesh is weak."[10]

Mary's parents were responsible but their inclination to spoil her is understandable. Their three other children died in infancy, leaving Mary as the center of their world and sole object of their affection. No wonder they were less strict than they should have been, and no wonder she became impulsive and temperamental. Still, there were compensating factors. She had a childlike reverence of nature and an artist's appreciation of its beauty. Ambition for wealth, power and social prestige did not exist in her and above all, like Elizabeth Barrett Browning, she adored her husband, loving him "to the depth and breadth and height [her] soul can reach."[11]

Lee returned that love in Mrs. Browning's same soul-reaching dimensions. His obvious enjoyment of pretty girls and handsome women might have caused whispered comments had not this fact been so apparent. But never was there a breath of scandal, for clearly Mary was the sun around which his world revolved. He saw the best and remained blind to the worst. In his eyes her virtues so outnumbered her vices that it never occurred to him to be embarrassed by her idiosyncrasies or to consider them prominent enough to need reform. She was who she was, and what she was, and he loved her as she was. Throughout their days each showed the other stars which had never been seen before. And each assisted in bearing the crosses laid upon the other.

*****

To be sure, friendship did not come easily to Lee but that fault was his alone for his natural grace, gentle nature and courteous manner made him attractive to men and women alike. One lady called him "The most noble looking mortal" she had ever seen and expressed the sentiment of everyone present when after his departure from a small gathering reflected, "We felt we had been visited by . . . royalty."[12] That was not an uncommon response, but he allowed only a few the familiarity of intimate friendship.

During the war years those closest to him were so much younger that their association was more a father-son relationship than a comfortable companionship of peers. Stonewall Jackson, for instance, was seventeen years his junior while Jeb Stuart was twenty-six years younger.

One who was a peer and close personal friend throughout their lives was his cousin, Cassius Lee, a childhood playmate and classmate at Mr. Hollowell's school in Alexandria. Having grown up together there were no secrets between them and no inhibitions. It was to Cassius he turned for help as a young man when searching for his family genealogy. His interest in the Virginia Theological Society was also heightened by Cassius's interest. Being possessed of the same strong faith, he did not hesitate at the outbreak of the war to discuss his Christian convocations and confide the prayerful hope that somehow God would bring victory to them in what had to be a one-sided conflict. Cassius was possibly the only civilian with whom he felt free to discuss military strategy and tactics. For example, Lee with unaccustomed frankness would explain that Jackson's failure to outflank McClellan's army during the Seven Days' Battle forced him to fight the Battle of Mechanicsville and that it was necessary to invade Maryland rather than attack Washington in 1862 because his army had not eaten for three days and could not have lasted long enough to lay siege against the city.[13] The life-long friendship between these two men was one of those homey associations which rewarded each of them with peace, relaxation, and mutual enjoyment.

Lee's closest friend at the U.S. Military Academy was Jack MacKay of Georgia. Jack was another with whom Lee felt free to air opinions. In 1833 when first he began to have mixed feelings about a military career it was to MacKay that he turned in discontent. He also shared secret feelings that garrison life offered too much freedom and too many opportunities for off-duty bottles and cards. A lot of concern was mixed in with no little disgust when he wrote . . . "it is a situation full of pains and one from which I shall modestly retire at the first fitting opportunity."[14]

Biographers are not agreed on the depth of friendship between Lee and his classmate, Joseph E. Johnston. "The Colonel" as Johnston was called during West Point days received his appointment to the academy immediately after Lee. He, too, was a Virginian and his father had fought under Light Horse Harry during the War for Independence. The two men had many common interests and were closely associated as cadets at Fort Monroe, in Washington, and in Mexico. But Johnston also possessed a driving ambition and ultra-conservative spirit. President Davis used to say that Johnston could not stand Lee beating him even in a game of billiards,[15] and he was not a little jealous of the advancement of others. Whether he resented Lee's advancement and permitted a one-sided rivalry to cool their friendship is difficult to determine but this much is certain—five years after the war they greeted each other like school boys in Savannah and posed for a pathetic last picture which portrays two old warriors who had fought too many battles and received too many mental and emotional wounds.

Others he counted as friends were Andrew Talcott of Connecticut, John A. Washington, who was killed early in western Virginia, and Walter S. Taylor, the handsome young man who served as his aide and in time as assistant adjutant general of the army.

Another young man named James Ewell Brown Stuart, a former classmate of Custis's at the academy, became one of his favorites. "Jeb" was a regular visitor in Superintendent Lee's home at West Point and on occasion at Arlington, for he had made his older friend into a father figure. When he was killed at Yellow Tavern, Lee covered his face and fled to his tent to hide his grief. Later in a General Order he stated sadly: "The mysterious hand of an all wise God has removed him from the scene of his usefulness . . . ."[16]

Lee and Jackson, despite the disparity in their years, had one of those special friendships which inspire the ages. The two men genuinely loved each other, though their personalities form a study in contrasts. Jackson, the zealous Presbyterian, prayed over a glass of water, was tormented by conscience when forced to fight on Sundays but otherwise loved a fight. Lee on the other hand was quietly reserved, serene of faith, and having done what he could to prepare for battle left the results to God. Jackson felt the power of God in his arm. Lee felt the love of God in heart. Jackson said he would follow Lee blindfolded while Lee returned the compliment saying, "I never troubled myself to give him detailed instructions. The most general suggestions were all that were needed."[17] All of his affection and admiration welled up after Jackson's death prompting him to explain to his brother, Carter, "I am grateful to Almighty God for having given us such a man."[18]

What Lee's friendships lacked in quantity was balanced by quality. At the end of his sixty-three years, they could be numbered on the fingers of his two hands but in every instance the love which characterized them went deep. As the *Book of Proverbs* teaches, "There is a friend that sticketh closer than a brother."[19] Lee was that kind of friend.

*****

Still it is in the fourth love — charity — by which he is especially identified. As in his ministry of reconciliation the downthrust from Heaven guided his outreach to man and in the process opened a new awareness of human value and kinship. As a result it was not duty but concern which motivated him. His heart could expand to encompass all mankind or contract to focus on one solitary individual. Over and over he proved that antagonisms, disagreements, and prejudice would not stifle such love.

During the war he was never quite able to separate many military enemies from friends. He found reasons to excuse and forgive the most flagrant behavior in that day. "Those people," as he liked to call the foe, were not only Americans, they were brothers who at their very worst were only temporary enemies. He may not have been that theological in his refusal to distinguish, but the Christ in his heart would not let him separate "them" from "us." In fact the "charity" he displayed during the Reconstruction period was no more virtuous than what he portrayed during the holocaust of war.

The assistance he gave to the widow of his old friend General Philip Kearney when he was killed at Chantilly,[20] and the good wishes he extended to the young Union soldier at Gettysburg who shouted, "Hurray for the Union," as he rode by are just two examples. As well as the cavalrymen under Colonel Ulric Dahlgren, against whom he refused to permit retaliation for their raid against Richmond, all point to the consistency with which he applied the love-ethic to the enemy. He left little doubt of his God-centeredness.

At the same time the love affair between him and his bittersweet army remain one of the most unprecedented in the annals of military history, for no commander stood higher in his regard for his men or theirs for him. As

Gamaliel Bradford reported, "Lee loved his army as if they were his children."[21] And the army returned the favor by extending him the affection and admiration of sons for their fathers.

There was the time he helped an uninhibited North Carolina infantryman find a plug of tobacco, and the consideration shown a very shy young artilleryman who had been invited to dine at a Southern home along with a group of high-ranking officers, and the pardon he granted a young husband who had deserted when his wife sent a complaining letter.

As General Gordon pointed out, "His unselfish solicitude for his men was marked and unvarying . . . He was the idealized commander of his army and at the same time the sympathizing brother of his men."[22]

Like Grace Church in Lexington, the congregation of St. Paul's Church in Richmond erected a memorial window which summed up his sacrificial devotion to soldier and civilian alike. The lower section depicts a young Moses taking leave of Pharaoh's court and casting from him the rod symbolizing his authority as a prince in Egypt's royal family. Beneath this portrayal is a text believed to have been chosen by his kinsman, Bishop Alfred R. Randolph:

> By faith Moses refused to be called the son of Pharaoh's daughter; Choosing rather to suffer affliction with the children of God for whom he endured as serving Him who is invisible.[23]

*****

Lee strove valiantly to emulate his Lord in a wholehearted love of his neighbor. Not only did he make a special effort to break through their protective facades and touch their hearts, he tried to see men and women as Christ saw them, to value them as He did, and to grant them the dignity and respect they deserved.

Willa Cather once wrote that, "Where there is great love there are always miracles."[24] Lee's consistent ability to give himself away, to forgive his enemies, and to exercise all the other functions of St. Paul's "charity" are convincing evidence of a great love which on more than one occasion did indeed border on the miraculous. Yet he would have been the first to agree with St. Augustine that, "All these gifts are of God. I did not give them to myself."[25]

The importance of self-denial and humility notwithstanding, the "loving kindness" described by the psalmist as being "better than life itself"[26] remains Lee's outstanding virtue. As has been noted, he and his family were one. And behind the Christian charity previously described was a Good Samaritan compulsion to bind up the wounds of any who had been beaten and robbed.

On the dreary journey to Richmond following his surrender, he came upon a young veteran whose mule had bolted leaving him to make his journey barefooted. Under the circumstances Lee might have been excused for passing by on the other side with a polite salute; instead, he stopped and exclaimed that the boy could not possibly make the long journey home without shoes. Then he took him to his brother Carter's house nearby and provided them.

CHAPTER TWELVE

Charisma

Historians are unanimously agreed that there was something majestic about Lee which set him apart and elevated him above ordinary men. But when they attempt to pinpoint this mystique, their findings and conclusions seldom bear any resemblance to each other.

Douglas S. Freeman, the South's foremost historian, insisted that Lee was exactly what he appeared to be, "a wholly human gentleman, the essential elements of whose positive character were two and two only, simplicity and spirituality."[1] Clifford Dowdey agreed, calling Lee "a simple man whose character grew in proportion to his commitment to the life-task he felt God had assigned him. . . ."[2] But Bruce Catton, the best narrator of the Union point of view, was of an opposite mind. He believed Lee was "one of the most profound enigmas of American life."[3] Another biographer, Thomas L. Connelley, who maintained no one went deep enough to examine Lee's soul, only went deep enough himself to call him, "a God figure for Virginians, a saint for the white Protestant South, and a hero for the nation."[4] Marshall W. Fishwick made an important distinction, saying "Lee's genius was essentially military; but his greatness was essentially religious."[5] All of them acknowledged Lee's greatness, but if they recognized the "How?" and "Why?" of God's contribution to it, they were hesitant to say so.

This was equally true of the contemporaries who worked alongside him or served under him. James C. Nisbet of Georgia wrote that "he was the only man I ever met who measured up to my concept of Washington. The grandeur of his appearance is beyond my power of portraiture. He is ineffable."[6] Alexander H. Stevens, vice-president of the Confederacy, admitted he was not one of Lee's early admirers and in the beginning "thought little enough of him anyhow." But after meeting him in Richmond, he reversed his opinion telling Jefferson Davis that the Virginian was "a David from the sheep-fold, in the pride of his manly beauty . . . the most manly man and entire gentleman I ever met.[7] Henry Adams, a Harvard classmate of Lee's son, Rooney, fell completely under his spell, and was forced to say, "He was simply beyond analysis; so simple that even the simple New England student could not realize him."[8] Mary Boykin Chesnut, on the other hand, thought his brother Smith was handsomer and more likeable. "Can anyone say they know his brother (Robert)?" she complained to her diary. "I doubt it. He looks so cold and grand."[9]

General John B. Gordon possessed the best literary talent in either army save possibly Union General Lew Wallace, who was to write *Ben Hur*. When he took his seat in the United States Senate following the war, Gordon said of Lee: "Like Niagara, the more you gazed the more his grandeur grew upon you, the more his majesty expanded and filled your spirit with a full satisfaction that left a perfect delight without the slightest feeling of oppression. Grandly majestic and dignified in all his deportment, he was genial as the sunlight in this beautiful day, and not a ray of that cordial, social intercourse but brought warmth to the heart as it did light to the understanding."[10]

Thus Lee's peers were struck by his appearance and personality and had no hesitancy in describing them. But even in that day when God was automatically, if often artificially, given credit for whatever was deemed good, those who knew him best seemed baffled by the spiritual forces which motivated him. It was a mystery which they failed to measure and apparently were incapable of identifying. The Reverend J. William Jones, a Baptist minister and close friend, almost solved it when he wrote: "If I have ever come in contact with a sincere devout Christian — one who seeing himself as a sinner, trusted alone in the merits of Christ, who humbly tried to walk the path of duty, 'Looking unto Jesus' as the author and finisher of his faith, and whose piety constantly exhibited itself in his daily life — that man was General Robert E. Lee."[11]

However, another Gordon, Edward Clifford Gordon, who was a temporary employee at the college while awaiting admission to a Presbyterian seminary, came closest to the truth by recognizing God's initiative. ". . . He is an epistle, written of God and designed by God to teach the people of this country that earthly success is not the criterion of merit, nor the measure of true greatness."[12]

Here is a picture which while referring to post-war conditions can be applied to most of Lee's adult life. ". . .written of God and designed by God . . ." are the key words. They speak directly to the activities of God in Lee's life and his ready response to them.

*****

What in fact this Southern hero possessed was a God-given *charisma*. It is popular today to describe any attractive person as having *charisma*, but the Christian meaning of the word is somewhat different. It is a unique form of grace, a radiant spirituality, that comes from God to set life aglow. This is the kind of grace which Lee received and which he communicated to all with whom he came in contact. Indeed, it was woven into his life like a symphonic theme whose melody lies beneath the surface yet breaks forth again and again to unite and characterize the complete work.

One of the most popular children's hymns in the Episcopal Church has lyrics written in 1929 by Lesbia Scott. They read:

> I sing a song of the saints of God
> Patient and brave and true
> Who toiled and fought and lived and died
> For the Lord they loved and knew . . .
> They loved their Lord so dear, so dear
> And his love made them strong
> And they followed the right for Jesus' sake,
> The whole of their good life long
> And one was a soldier . . .[13]

Few lines are more applicable to the life of Robert E. Lee. All his inherited qualities are there to enhance his nobility. Acquired values including devotion to duty and discipline are also there. Nevertheless, although a soldier, nothing is more certain than that God's love entered that part of him which was governed neither by heredity nor environment. And it was there! That is the only explanation that passes muster.

It seems the greatest exaggeration and almost a blasphemy to suggest that when Lee looked at people and they looked at him, somehow they felt compelled to become what he expected them to be. However, this occurred not only with individuals but on several occasions with large bodies of men.

His biographer, Gamaliel Bradford, could write, "I have loved Lee, and I may say that his influence upon my own life has been as deep and as inspiring as any I have ever known."[14] An artilleryman said, "We loved him much but revered him more."[15] A trooper exclaimed, "We knew very well that he was only a man . . . but practically we believed nothing of the kind." When some ragamuffin men were waiting in Richmond for transportation back to the front and learned that he was at that moment saying his prayers for them at St. Paul's, they rushed to the church for a glimpse of him as one of them exclaimed, "God bless him. God bless his dear old soul."[16]

A few days after Appomattox a Union soldier who had served under him in Texas appeared at the doorstep of his Franklin Street residence in Richmond with a basket of food. On his departure he attempted to embrace and kiss his former commander, saying "Goodbye Colonel! God bless ye! If I could have gotten over in time I would have been with ye!"[17] Then as one of his students at Lexington said, ". . . he had a power to bring out, and did bring out, the very best that was in every student."[18] Always it was people's faith in him and their faith in his faith, which like magnets drew them to him and to that mysterious force — *charisma.*

Entire divisions of soldiers were similarly affected. After the Battle of Chancellorsville, an unplanned and unaccountable demonstration was accorded him in which the feeble cries of the wounded joined the fierce rebel yells of the combatants to break every bond of emotional restraint. Beginning with one small unit, the shout was picked up by regiment after regiment until thousands of voices were roaring their tribute in unison to their commander. In recording the event one of his staff said, ". . . I thought it must have been from such a scene that men in ancient times rose to the dignity of gods."[19] In part, the desire to celebrate their victory sparked the spontaneous praise, but beyond that was the sheer joy felt at being in the presence of the one responsible for it. Like an electric shock it passed through the entire army, awakening all present to an at oneness with a revered leader who had become the living symbol of their cause.

When General James Longstreet's corps returned to the Army of Northern Virginia after several futile months in the west, Lee rode out to meet it. The men were lined at attention, rank on rank, and a bugle sounded to announce his arrival. Out to the center of the line he cantered on Traveler and turned to face them. He did not say a word. He simply looked at them and slowly removed his hat. The result was pandemonium. Years later one of those present said, "[T]he effect was as of a military sacrament."[20]

Not even defeat could destroy the almost religious reverence his men felt for him. At Gettysburg with twenty Confederate battle flags scattered over a hundred yard to signify the repulse, his men insisted, "Uncle Robert will get us into Washington yet; you bet he will."[21] When after the war he visited Jacksonville, Florida, on the riverboat *Nick King*, there was the same devotion but a different expression of it. As he appeared on deck, a complete silence fell over the hundreds who awaited him there, and it continued unbroken while they gazed in admiration at their venerated chief.

His visit to Baltimore to promote the building of the railroad to the Valley of Virginia produced a similar result. Not only was he greeted wildly by a huge throng on the floor of the Corn and Flour Exchange; when it was learned he was attending services at St. Paul's Episcopal Church that Sunday, a large number of admirers collected outside to await his appearance. When he came through the door, every man present removed his hat and remained uncovered until he passed through a line which extended some distance down the street.

The emotion-charged surrender at Appomattox could not be expected to be different. In spite of an effort at formality, Lee's famous Order No. 9 contained all the pathos of a fallen leader's farewell to his men, and left undisguised the admiration and affection he held for them. While prepared by his aide, Colonel Charles Marshall, the order was carefully edited by him, and his very soul was in it as he spoke.

"After four years of arduous service, marked by unsurpassed courage and fortitude, the Army of Northern Virginia has been compelled to yield to overwhelming numbers and resources.

"I need not tell the brave survivors of so many hard fought battles, who have remained steadfast to the last, that I have consented to the result from no distrust of them.

"But feeling that valor and devotion could accomplish nothing that would compensate for the loss that must have attended the continuance of the contest, I determined to avoid the useless sacrifice of these whose past services have endeared them to their countrymen . . .

"With an increasing admiration for your constancy and devotion to your country, and a grateful remembrance of your kind and generous consideration for myself, I bid you all an affectionate farewell."[22]

His wasted troops greeted the announcement with unabashed sadness, crying their willingness to follow him anywhere, insisting, "We'll fight 'em yet,"[23] and, "I love you just as well as ever General Lee."[24] During the hours which followed, with tears streaming down their cheeks, his dirty, ragged men pressed about him seeking to touch him, or his stirrups, or his horse. They could not let him go. Finally, despite every effort, Lee succumbed to his own feelings. With head uncovered he walked Traveler through the mass of weeping, cheering men, bowing acknowledgment and making no effort to hide the tears that were staining his cheeks.

Of course it can be argued that such an emotional response would be natural under the circumstances, but the argument does not satisfy all the facts. There was an intangible spiritual commitment which went deeper than fleeting emotion. Loyalty to their commander not only carried his men to heights beyond their normal capacities, it moved them to sacrifice themselves freely even after they knew they could not win. Only the magnetic influence of his God-given *charisma* could account for such devotion.

*****

Not only did this spiritual gift move soldier and civilian to identify with Lee, it moved him in his quiet way to identify with them. Every inch an aristocrat, cultured, educated, gentle and courteous, he was in no way comparable to many of his tobacco-chewing, whiskey-drinking, profane and ill-mannered men, not a few of whom could not write their names. Yet while standing apart from them in this respect, he assumed their lifestyles with an affection neither rank nor culture could resist.

Colonel Walter Taylor said his commander had a private soldier's simplicity in his dislike of parades, ceremonies, and gold braid. Certainly he insisted upon a small staff and bluntly refused every effort on the part of lieutenants to provide him with the traditional escort or guard of honor due a commanding general. Sometimes his headquarters were reduced to a single tent which he and his aide-de-camp shared at night as well as day when unexpected visitors arrived. Throughout the war his dinner service was tin plates, cups and bowls, scarcely better than those issued to men in the ranks, except, for one short period when members of his staff insisted on borrowing some china for his table.

Such insistence on living the life his army was living, was incomprehensible to military observers from other lands. Colonel Garnet Wolseley of England, later Field Marshal Viscount Wolseley, could not refrain from commenting on the total lack of camp comforts so characteristic of European commanders. But Lee's butternut army saw his desire to share their privations and endure what they were forced to endure, and this increased their love for him.

An additional reason for living under canvas rather than in a comfortable home was a fear of enemy reprisal against those who entertained him. Union General John Pope, for instance, was on record with the threat to arrest all male civilians behind the lines who refused to take the oath of allegiance. Those who communicated with the enemy, even so much as by a family letter, were to be considered spies. Consequently, in many instances Lee not only refused his countrymen's courtesies, he even forbade his tent to be pitched in their front yards. It was the kind of thoughtfulness which gave non-combatants additional cause to love him.

His desire to share what his men endured and his concern to protect the unprotected provided an excellent example for all concerned, appealing to the best natures of soldiers and civilians alike and reminding them of their obligations to consider one another.

Naturally the pride and love they bore for their military leader soon led them to identify the Army of Northern Virginia with him. It became "Lee's Army," "Lee's Waders" (from the river crossing after Gettysburg), and "Lee's Miserables" after Victor Hugo's novel which was being widely read at the time. Civilians called it "Mr. Lee's Army." When war came to an end and he had adjourned to Washington College, correspondence from those who did not know the name of the institution, or did not care, was in like fashion addressed to "Mr. Lee's College," or "General Lee's School." Such mail was always delivered!

Colonel Wolseley was close to the truth when he reported, "While all honor him, those with whom he was most intimate felt for him the affection of sons for a father."[25] That feeling was, however, far more widespread than a selected number of intimate associates. It is difficult to describe people's reverence for him, and as noted, sometimes more difficult to believe.

Although unconsciously, Lee strengthened the parental image the South had for him by his continuing concern for others. Had he chosen to do so, he could have led them into further bloodshed with guerrilla warfare following his retreat from Petersburg. Had he been a different kind of man, he could have used them for political advancement. Had ambition rather than affection guided him, he could have forsaken them for wealth, prestige and comfort in another land. However, from the moment he accepted his commission in the Confederate Army to that fatal October day in 1870 he sought to be at one with them.

They in turn made him the symbol of an idealized day which they thought they remembered, but which by fire and blood was now gone with the wind. He was their "Representative man, who as Robert Lacey wrote of King George V, pictured for them life not as much as it was, but life as most of them wished it still might be.[26] More than that, they made him the heartbeat upon whom the South depended for survival. If true greatness includes the ability to identify with and be representative of one's people, then Lee with his *Charisma* unquestionably qualifies.

*****

But there was that within Lee which could never be content as a "representative man," for in his life as in his military strategy he was conditioned to attack. More precisely, the role in which circumstances cast him and the grace with which God empowered him taught that representation without leadership could amount to stagnation or worse. It is a lesson that those in public service would do well to remember for to be at one with others is beneficial only when the oneness is a means of opening their eyes to wider visions and spurring their hearts to greater goals. St. Paul was aware of this for he cautioned the Corinthians, "If the trumpet gives an uncertain sound, who shall prepare for the battle?"[27]

There was nothing uncertain about the sounds of Lee's trumpet on the battlefield of the spirit. He was an authentic Christian who exemplified the highest level of goodness and inspired his peers, their children, and their children's children to go and do likewise. He was in fact a special kind of "representative" who took a bit of Heaven with him wherever he went. From his Mexican days to his terminal illness in Lexington he wrote, spoke and acted according to his trust in "the gifts of a merciful God."

Early each morning he focused his attention and that of his family upon their Creator. He never lost an opportunity to show that in God alone lay salvation. As the *Alexandria Gazette* said even before he donned Confederate gray, "his chivalric character, his probity, honor, and—we may say to his eternal praise—his Christian life and conduct—make his very name a 'tower of strength.'"[28]

Such was his integrity that he took special care even to avoid the appearance of nepotism. When his wife Mary expressed anxiety for the safety of their youngest son and suggested his appointment to his father's staff, Lee replied, "I should prefer Rob's being in the line, in an independent position, where he could rise by his own merit and not through the recommendation of his relatives."[29] When Rob approached him about his need for a new pair of shoes, his father inquired whether the other men in his battery had received theirs. On being informed they had not, he suggested that Rob wait to obtain his through regular channels. And when, a Federal general in Libby Prison at Richmond requested a special exchange between himself and the imprisoned Rooney, Lee answered that he could not ask for his son "a favor which could not be asked for the humblest soldier in the army."[30]

Refusals to favor his flesh and blood did not deter him from worrying about them, however. He was first of all a father when he noted Rooney had gone out in the rain without his overcoat. He was as concerned over Custis's discontent with his unimpressive post as a military aide to President Davis, and when eighteen-year-old Rob was struggling with the decision to enlist in the army, he offered daily prayer that a loving God would guide him. His grief over Charlotte's death was a double portion, for he knew what agony her loss would cost Rooney. The obligation to lead created a compulsory acceptance of certain priorities, but it did not make blind his love for his children.

The tone he set after the war at Washington College was equally clear. "The first business of education," he said, "is to draw forth and put into habitual exercise the former dispositions, such as kindness, justice, and self-denial."[31] To that end he introduced the honor system and made it the student's responsibility to behave like gentlemen. One member of the student body remarked that they did so, "not because they feared [him but because they] loved him." He added, "I don't think there was one of the boys . . . but would have died defending him if necessary."[32] The thought was supported by a Lexington clergyman who insisted, "No college in the land had . . . a better behaved, more orderly set of students."[33] In 1870, records show that of all the students enrolled, only six were subject to any form of discipline.

It has been noted how realistic Lee was in recognizing the need for a curriculum which could prepare the students of that day to earn their daily bread. Although a firm believer in classical education under ordinary circumstances, he knew that young Southerners were untrained in many fields which required special preparation. So he promoted a business school; introduced courses in Spanish because of the nearness to Mexico; asked a professor of applied mathematics to lay the groundwork for a School of Engineering; upgraded "Natural Philosophy" and divided it into its main subjects, chemistry and physics; and arranged for the Lexington Law School to become affiliated with the college. Five new professorships were created and contributions towards scholarships were earnestly sought. The *New York Herald* visualized this reorganization as "practical education" and stated that Lee "was likely to make as great an impression upon our old fogy schools and colleges as . . . in military tactics [he did] upon our old fogy commanders in the palmy days of the rebellion."[34]

His trumpet was never more certain than in off-campus efforts to rally the South around the Stars and Stripes again. Marching once at the head of a column of Virginia Military Institute cadets with their superintendent in Lexington, he purposely refrained from keeping in step. It was just another way to remind those who were watching that the war was over, and he was a civilian like all the others who had worn a Confederate uniform.

The Reverend J. William Jones approached him one day just as an ill-clad man was taking his leave. "That is one of our old soldiers who is in necessitous circumstances," Lee explained. When Jones inquired about the man's regiment, Lee admitted, "He fought on the other side, but we must not remember that against him now." He did not tell the Baptist minister that he had helped his visitor financially.[35]

Always, Lee preached moderation and hope. It was his rule to answer every one of the anxious letters which came by the bushel, and wherever indicated, to counsel forbearance. His prophesies of a new day when the vindictive powers in Washington would be replaced by a more lenient and understanding Congress were constant. His announced intention to remain in Virginia verified that conviction. And the model he set regarding obedience to constituted authority was a major contribution to the reinstatement of former government.

In such ways he offered leadership as well as representation and in time Southerners began to accept and follow it. They applauded his understanding of human nature, and concluded reluctantly that there was merit even in his belief that the North would eventually rectify the injustices of the Reconstruction acts. The sound of his trumpet led a battered people to the discovery of a new spirit and a fresh energy with which to rebuild their lives. Surely this, too, stands as a signal mark of his *charisma* and his greatness.

*****

According to the late Walter Russell Bowie, the test of true religion is *"whether or not it is producing the kind of life in which the beauty of God appears."*[36] By that standard Robert E. Lee's spirituality is validated on all counts. The beauty of God can be seen in his endless pursuit of righteousness. It is apparent in the spotlessness of his character. It shows from the clearly marked guidelines which he set to direct Christian behavior for his and every generation.

He received the widest acclaim for his achievements as a military leader, and an admiration bordering on idolatry as the custodian of Southern ideals, but it was by the hand of God and the gift of *charisma* that he was able to become who he was, and accomplish what he did. Stanley Horn, a long time student of Lee's life, has pointed out that "the fame of but a few soldiers have survived such failure as he experienced." But he continued with the explanation that Lee's fame lies in his character, "in his greatness as a man," and in "such high ideals and principles that his whole conduct was governed by them."[37] In short, Lee's greatness lies in his response to the initiative of a loving God and to the faith it supplied.

NOTES

Preface

1. Connelly, *The Marble Man*, p. 163.
2. Marshall, *The Life of George Washington*, vol. 5, p. xiii.

Chapter One

1. Marshall, vol. 5, p. 767.
2. Her name was originally spelled Anne, but the "e" was dropped.
3. I John 5:4.
4. Freeman, *R. E. Lee*, vol. 1, p. 30.
5. Ibid.
6. Ibid., p. 27.
7. Dowdey, *Lee*, p. 42. Lee's future mother-in-law was Fitzhugh's sister.
8. Ibid., p. 43.
9. Mrs. G. W. P. Carter was one of Meade's early friends and advisors.
10. Freeman, *R. E. Lee*, vol. 1, p. 28.
11. Jones, *Christ in the Camp*, p. 69.
12. The requirement was continued up to the 1979 edition of the *Book of Common Prayer*.
13. Freeman, *George Washington*, vol. 6, p. xliii.
14. Freeman, *R. E. Lee*, vol. 1, p. 40.
15. Ibid., p. 46.
16. Three others died in infancy.
17. Inge, *Personal Religion and the Life of Devotion*, p. 45.
18. Hebrews 11:1.

Chapter Two

1. Trueblood, *Abraham Lincoln: Theologian of American Anguish*, p. 76.
2. Matthew 11:28.
3. Matthew 15:25.
4. Freeman, *R. E. Lee*, vol. 1, p. 172.
5. George Bernard Shaw, *Collected Plays*, p. 864.
6. Lee, Jr., *Recollections and Letters of General Robert E. Lee*, p. 143.
7. Riegel and Haigh, *History of the United States*, p. 331.
8. Freeman, *R. E. Lee*, vol. 1, pp. 247–48.

9. He never forgot his protege's record and years later in 1861 was to recommend him for command of the Federal troops recruited for the invasion of the South.

10. Freeman, *R. E. Lee*, vol. 1, p. 249.

11. Ibid., p. 135.

12. Connelly, *The Marble Man*, pp. 181–82.

13. Flood, *Lee, The Last Years*, p. 3.

14. Dowdey, *Lee*, p. 573.

15. *Battles and Leaders of the Civil War*, vol. 4, p. 240.

16. Ibid.

17. Fishwick, *Lee After the War*, p. 92.

18. Freeman, *R. E. Lee*, vol. 2, p. 488.

19. This young courier was James Steptoe Johnson, the future bishop of the Episcopal diocese of West Texas.

20. Her father was the grandson of Martha Washington and Washington's adopted son.

21. Hood, *Advance and Retreat*, p. 8.

22. Shaara, *The Killer Angels*, p. 54.

23. "Christian Soldier," anonymous, p. 194.

Chapter Three

1. Fishwick, *Robert E. Lee: Churchman*, p. 5.

2. The *Hymnal of the Episcopal Church*, 1982, #689.

3. Cf. Micklem, *This Is Our Faith*, p. 55.

4. Lee, Jr., *Recollections and Letters*, p. 39.

5. Ibid., p. 96.

6. Ibid., p. 305.

7. The *Book of Common Prayer*, 1979, p. 868.

8. Lee, *To Markie*, p. 65.

9. Fishwick, *Lee After the War*, p. 213.

10. Jones, *Christ in the Camp*, p. 65.

11. Ibid., p. 64.

12. Connelly, *The Marble Man*, pp. 181–82.

13. Freeman, *R. E. Lee*, vol. 4, p. 270.

14. Jones, *Christ in the Camp*, p. 61.

15. Freeman, *R. E. Lee*, vol. 3, p. 531. Jones gives a less probable version in *Christ in Camp*, p. 53, saying the exchange of prayer books was between Lee and a Richmond book salesman.

16. His copy, which is at the Confederate Museum in Richmond, is marked at Psalm 120, "When I was in trouble I called upon the Lord." It is not known who marked the passage.

17. *Somebody's Darling* was used most effectively in the cinema version of *Gone With the Wind*.

18. Yet he once said, "Without music we could not have an army."

19. The *Hymnal*, 1982, #636. There were six stanzas in Lee's 1845 version, but the 5th promising loving care for the elderly was dropped later. Other reductions also were made.

20. Psalms 31:17.

21. C. S. Lewis, *Surprised by Joy*, p. 237.

22. Burnett, ed., *The Spirit of Man*, "My Religion."

23. Lee, Jr., *Recollections and Letters*, p. 6.

24. MacDonald, *Mrs. Robert E. Lee*, p. 117. See also Proverbs 8:17.

Chapter Four

1. Quoted by Ralph W. Sockman, *The Higher Happiness*, p. 149.

2. The *Book of Common Prayer*, 1979, p. 856.

3. Acts 9:6.

4. Freeman, *R. E. Lee*, vol. 1, p. 417.

5. Ibid., pp. 1, 4.

6. It is possible this statement was prompted by the advice George Washington offered his nephews in willing them his swords. Never draw your blade from their scabbards, he wrote, save in self-defense or the defense of your country. Freeman, *R. E. Lee*, vol. 1, p. 467.

7. Matthew 15:25.

8. Psalms 84:6.

9. Lee, Jr., *Recollections and Letters*, pp. 79–80.

10. John 17:15.

11. Jones, *Christ in the Camp*, p. 52.

12. Ibid., p. 60.

13. Jones, *Life and Letters of Robert Edward Lee*, p. 79.

14. Lee, Jr., *Recollections and Letters*, p. 16.

15. Ibid.

16. Ibid., p. 94.

17. Ibid.

18. Jones, *Life and Letters of Robert Edward Lee*, pp. 210–11.

19. Fishwick, *Lee After the War*, pp. 210–11.

20. Matthew 18:20.

21. The *Hymnal,* 1940, #495.

22. Quoted by Paul Schearer in *For We Have This Treasure*, p. 141.

23. Douglas, *I Rode With Stonewall*, p. 155.

24. Lee, Jr., *Recollections and Letters*, p. 405.

Chapter Five

1. *The Book of Common Prayer*, 1789.

2. Freeman, *R. E. Lee*, vol. 1, p. 331.

3. The Vietnam War was an exception and to a lesser degree so was the war with Korea. This "compromise ethic" will be treated in greater detail in the next chapter.

4. Shepherd, Jr., *The American Prayer Book Commentary,* pp. v–vi.

5. Freeman, *R. E. Lee*, vol. 1, p. 439.

6. Clebach, *The Church and the Confederate States,* pp. 1–20.

7. Ibid., p. 126.

8. Here again the "religious grounds" were the invasion of the South and the call to neighboring states to provide troops for this purpose.

9. Weddell, *St. Paul's Church, (Richmond)*, vol. 1, pp. 145–47.

10. Lee, Jr., *Recollections and Letters*, p. 56.

11. Ibid., p. 248.

12. Fishwick, *Lee After the War,* p. 218.

13. Lee, Jr., *Recollections and Letters*, p. 418.

14. Dowdey, *Lee*, p. 731.

15. Flood, *Lee, The Last Years*, p. 157.

16. Ibid., p. 261.

17. II Timothy 4:7.

Chapter Six

1. Kaufman, *The Theological Imagination*, p. 274.

2. Mark 14:15.

3. Matthew 10:29–30.

4. Bradford, *Lee, The American*, p. 246.

5. Freeman, *R. E. Lee*, vol. 1, p. 369–70.

6. Lee, Jr., *Recollections and Letters*, p. 75.

7. Freeman, *R. E. Lee*, vol. 3, p. 1.

8. Lee, *To Markie*, p. 101.

9. Dowdey and Manarin, *Wartime Papers*, p. 547.

10. Lee, Jr., *Recollections and Letters*, p. 151.

11. Dowdey and Manarin, *Wartime Papers*, p. 429.

12. Freeman, *R. E. Lee*, vol. 3, p. 55.

13. Dowdey and Manarin, *Wartime Papers*, p. 551.

14. Jones, *Christ in the Camp*, p. 56.

15. Freeman, *R. E. Lee*, vol. 4, p. 194.

16. Temple, "The Centrality of Christ," p. 41.

17. Bayne, "Now is the Accepted Time," p. 38.

18. John 10:30.

19. Matthew 17:5.

20. Matthew 5:6.

21. Jones, *Christ in the Camp*, p. 60.

22. I Corinthians 2:10.

23. Quote from Bowie, *The Master*, p. 17.

24. Matthew 1:21.

25. John 8:11.

26. Luke 23:24.

27. Jones, *Personal Reminiscences, Anecdotes, and Letters of General Robert E. Lee.*

28. The *Book of Common Prayer*, 1865, p. 248.

29. The *Hymnal*, 1982, #167.

30. Lee, Jr., *Recollections and Letters*, p. 80.

31. Jones, *Christ in the Camp*, p. 68.

32. John 3:16.

33. John 14:16.

34. John 16:13.

35. Acts 2:31.

36. The *Book of Common Prayer*, 1865, p. 248.

37. Ibid., p. 11.

38. Ibid., p. 207.

39. Lee, Jr., *Recollections and Letters*, p. 183.

40. Jones, *Christ in the Camp*, p. 77.

41. Freeman, *R. E. Lee*, vol. 4, p. 298, fn. 119.

42. Luke 15 ff.

43. Cf. chapter eleven.

44. Freeman, *R. E. Lee*, vol. 4, p. 483.

45. The *Book of Common Prayer*, 1865, p. 392.

46. Fishwick, *Lee After the War*, p. 213.

Chapter Seven

1. Hammarskjold, *Markings*, p. 122.

2. Lee, *To Markie*, p. 66.

3. Proverbs 22:1.

4. Freeman, *R. E. Lee*, vol. 1, p. 31.

5. Lee, *Lee of Virginia*, p. 346.

6. Freeman, *George Washington*, vol. 2, p. 204.

7. Ibid., vol. 3, XI.

8. Mason, *Popular Life of Robert Edward Lee*, p. 225.

9. *Battles and Leaders*, vol. 2, p. 277.

10. Fishwick, *Lee After the War*, p. 98.

11. Freeman, *R. E. Lee*, vol. 4, p. 464.

12. Aurelius, *Meditations*.

13. Long, *Memoirs of Robert E. Lee*, p. 485.

14. Ibid., p. 486.

15. Ibid., p. 464.

16. Lee, Jr., *Recollections and Letters*, p. 139.

17. Ibid., p. 303.

18. Freeman, *R. E. Lee*, vol. 1, p. 410.

19. Lee, *To Markie*, pp. 36–37.

20. Ibid., p. 57.

21. Lee, Jr., *Recollections and Letters*, p. 205.

22. Freeman, *R. E. Lee*, vol. 4, p. 505.

23. Ibid., p. 270.

24. Ibid., vol. 1, p. 343.

25. Ibid., vol. 4, p. 279.

26. Proverbs 23:7.

27. Jones, *Personal Reminiscences*, p. 319.

28. Dowdey and Manarin, *Wartime Papers*, p. 400.

29. Matthew 18:3.

30. Temple, *Christian, Faith and Life*, p. 111.

31. Freeman, *R. E. Lee*, vol. 1, p. 48.

32. Freeman, *R. E. Lee*, vol. 2, p. 420.

33. Lee, *General Lee*, p. 171.

34. Jones, *Personal Reminiscences*, p. 368.

35. Ibid., p. 369.

36. Ibid.

37. Jones, *Life and Letters*.

38. Ephesians 6:13.

39. Gordon, *Reminiscences of the Civil War*, p. 232.

40. Dowdey, *Lee*, p. 734.

Chapter Eight

1. Eliot, *Selected Essays*, p. 367.

2. Luke 18:9–14.

3. Long, *Memoirs*, p. 486.

4. Jones, *Personal Reminiscences*, p. 148.

5. Ibid., p. 295; Jones, *Life and Letters*.

6. Sanborn, *Robert E. Lee: The Complete Man*, p. 213.

7. Ibid., p. 113.

8. Connelly, *The Marble Man*, p. 49.

9. McCabe, Jr., *General Robert E. Lee*, vol. 1, p. 316.

10. Ibid., pp. 178–79.

11. Sanburg, *Abraham Lincoln: The War Years*, vol. 2, p. 80.

12. Flood, *Lee, The Last Years*, pp. 56, 152.

13. I Corinthians 13:4.

14. Matthew 11:29.

15. Sanborn, *Robert E. Lee: The Complete Man*, p. 116.

16. Long, *Memoirs*, p. 229.

17. Ibid., pp. 240–41.

18. Hood, *Advance and Retreat*, p. 51.

19. Lee, *To Markie*, p. 11.

20. Ibid., p. 14.

21. Lee, Jr., *Recollections and Letters*, pp. 200–201.

22. Long, *Memoirs*, p. 401.

23. Maury, *Recollections of a Virginian*.

24. Fishwick, *Lee After the War*, p. 88.

25. Long, *Memoirs*, p. 433.

26. Jones, *Life and Letters*, p. 86.

27. Lee, Jr., *Recollections and Letters*, p. 15.

28. MacDonald, *Mrs. Robert E. Lee*, pp. 115–16.

29. Long, *Memoirs*, p. 465.

30. Lee, Jr., *Recollections and Letters*, p. 88.

31. Matthew 10:16.

32. Freeman, *R. E. Lee*, vol. 4, p. 483.

33. Lee, *To Markie*, p. 100.

34. Ibid., p. 116.

35. Romans 8:35.

36. *Leaves of Gold: An Anthology*, p. 145.

Chapter Nine

1. Charles Anderson's brother, Robert, was commanding Fort Sumter when the match was put to the powder barrel.

2. Freeman, *R. E. Lee*, vol. 1, p. 420.

3. Sandburg, *Abraham Lincoln*, vol. 6, p. 94.

4. Sandburg, *Abraham Lincoln*, vol. 1, p. 590.

5. Latourette, *A History of Christianity*, p. 1007.

6. The *Book of Common Prayer*, 1789, p. 848.

7. Ibid., p. 875. (Cf. also the original 1571 and 1662 text of this article.)

8. Romans 13:7-8.

9. Sanborn, *Robert E. Lee: The Complete Man*, p. 125.

10. Freeman, *R. E. Lee*, vol. 1, p. 376.

11. McCabe, Jr., *The Life and Campaigns of General Robert E. Lee*, p. 383.

12. Price, *Civil War Handbook*, p. 17.

13. Mark 12:17.

14. Dowdey, *Lee*, p. 396.

15. Niebuhr, *The Nature and Destiny of Man*, vol. 1, pp. 283-84.

16. Freeman, *R. E. Lee*, vol. 2, p. 481.

17. Mason, *Popular Life of General Robert E. Lee*, p. 211.

18. Freeman, *R. E. Lee*, vol. 1, p. 383.

19. Fishwick, *Robert E. Lee: Churchman*, p. 19.

20. Lee, *To Markie*, p. 67.

21. Lee was 32 years of age when rail transportation began to operate in Pennsylvania and 37 when Samuel F. G. Morse first signaled by telegraph "what hath God wrought."

22. Price, *Civil War Handbook*, p. 17.

23. Lee, Jr., *Recollections and Letters*, pp. 88-89.

24. Gordon, *Reminiscences of the Civil War*, p. 460.

25. Infra, chapter 11, fn. 13.

26. Sandburg, *Abraham Lincoln*, vol. 6, p. 211.

27. Freeman, *R. E. Lee*, vol. 4, p. 401.

28. Ibid., vol. 1, p. 372.

29. Earle, "Pictorial Life of Robert E. Lee," pp. 102-3.

30. Freeman, *R. E. Lee*, vol. 1, p. 417.

31. Ibid., p. 364.

32. Lee, Jr., *Recollections and Letters*, pp. 168, 306.

33. Latourette, *A History of Christianity*, p. 1251. Gunnary Mydral suggests lower figures in *An American Dilemma*, p. 860.

34. Mason, *Popular Life*, p. 60.

35. Craton, *History of the Bahamas*, pp. 205-6.

36. Freeman, *R. E. Lee*, vol. 1, p. 372.

37. MacDonald, *Mrs. Robert E. Lee*, p. 100.

Chapter Ten

1. Ephesians 2:14.

2. II Corinthians 5:18.

3. Fishwick, *Lee After the War*, p. 12.

4. "Scalawags" was the name given native Southerners who remained quiet during the conflict but rose up in search of benefits once Union troops occupied the land.

5. *Fairfax County: A History*, pp. 372-73, by county supervisors.

6. Freeman, *R. E. Lee*, vol. 1, p. 292.

7. Sanburg, *Abraham Lincoln*, vol. 4, p. 94.

8. Flood, *Lee, The Last Years*, p. 60.

9. Fishwick, *Lee After the War*, p. 16.

10. Commager, *America's Robert E. Lee*, p. 110.
11. Ibid., p. 111.
12. Sanburg, *Abraham Lincoln*, vol. 4, p. 218.
13. Flood, *Lee, The Last Years*, p. 88.
14. Ibid.
15. Dowdey, *Lee*, p. 623.
16. Freeman, *R. E. Lee*, vol. 4, p. 317. See also Dowdey's *Lee*, pp. 622–25, for a further treatment of this subject.
17. Fishwick, *Lee After the War*, p. 125.
18. Ibid., p. 68.
19. Bond, *Memories*, p. 19.
20. Flood, *Lee, The Last Years*, p. 58.
21. Ibid., p. 56.
22. Long, *Memoirs*, p. 457.
23. Dowdey, *Lee*, p. 611.
24. Ibid., p. 684.
25. Ibid., p. 630.
26. Lee, Jr., *Recollections and Letters*, p. 253.
27. Ibid., p. 359.
28. In point of fact the parole which he signed April 9, 1865 contained no oath of allegiance but only a promise not to serve in any military capacity against the United States.
29. Freeman, *R. E. Lee*, vol. 4, pp. 200–206.
30. Flood, *Lee, The Last Years*, p. 100. See also pp. 63 and 276 for further treatment of the subject. Lee's citizenship was restored posthumously by a Senate Joint Resolution and signed into law by President Ford on August 4, 1975.
31. Lee, Jr., *Recollections and Letters*, p. 163.
32. Freeman, *R. E. Lee*, vol. 4, p. 236.
33. Jones, *Personal Reminiscences*, p. 323.
34. Ibid., p. 234.
35. Flood, *Lee, The Last Years*, p. 136.
36. Stern, *Robert E. Lee: The Man and Soldier*, pp. 230–31.
37. Freeman, *R. E. Lee*, vol. 4, p. 257.
38. Lee, Jr., *Recollections and Letters*, pp. 224–25.
39. *Fairfax County: A History*, contributors, p. 379.
40. Freeman, *R. E. Lee*, vol. 4, pp. 313–14.
41. Ibid., vol. 4, p. 220.
42. Dowdey, *Lee*, p. 599.

Chapter Eleven

1. I John 4:8.
2. II Corinthians 6:6.
3. Lewis, *The Four Loves*, pp. 176 ff, lists these loves as affection, friendship, physical love, and charity.
4. Henry Lee's body was moved later to the chapel at Washington and Lee University where his son and other family members are buried.
5. As Rob wrote: "They were dedicated to each other, having always kept their small boyish love." Lee, Jr., *Recollections and Letters*, p. 362.

6. Freeman, *R. E. Lee*, vol. 1, p. 196.
7. Ibid., vol. 4, p. 392.
8. Lee, Jr., *Recollections and Letters*, p. 247.
9. Ibid., p. 252.
10. Freeman, *R. E. Lee*, vol. 1, p. 108.
11. Browning, *Sonnets from the Portuguese*, p. XLIII.
12. Jones, *A Rebel War Clerk's Diary*, vol. 1, p. 125.
13. Freeman, *R. E. Lee*, vol. 4, pp. 474-75.
14. Ibid., vol. 1, p. 122.
15. Strode, *Jefferson Davis: Tragic Hero*, vol. 2, pp. 79–80.
16. Dowdey, *The Wartime Papers of R. E. Lee*, p. 736.
17. Freeman, *R. E. Lee*, vol. 2, p. 562.
18. Ibid., vol. 3, p. 1.
19. Proverbs 18:24.
20. Sometimes called "Ox Hill."
21. Bradford, *Lee, The American*, p. 79.
22. Gordon, *Reminiscences of the Civil War*, pp. 230–31.
23. Hebrews 11:24.
24. Cather, *Death Comes for the Archbishop*, p. 50.
25. Augustine, *Confessions*, p. 18.
26. Psalm 63:3.

Chapter Twelve

1. Freeman, *R. E. Lee*, vol. 4, p. 494.
2. Dowdey, *Lee*, p. xi.
3. Connelly, *The Marble Man*, p. 163.
4. Ibid., p. 3.
5. Fishwick, *Lee After the War*, p. 228.
6. Nisbet, *Four Years on the Firing Line*, p. 109.
7. Strode, *Jefferson Davis*, p. 62.
8. Fishwick, *Lee After the War*, p. 227.
9. Earle, *Robert E. Lee*, p. 69.
10. The original of this quotation is said to have been delivered on the floor of the U.S. Senate but a search of the *Congressional Record* has failed to uncover it. The author's source is a longhand version written by a Confederate veteran in a volume of Gordon's *Reminiscences*.
11. Jones, *Christ in the Camp*, p. 81.
12. Hood, *Lee, the Final Years*, p. 214.
13. The *Hymnal*, 1982, #293.
14. Fishwick, *Lee After the War*, p. 225.
15. Sanborn, *Robert E. Lee: The Complete Man*, p. 82.
16. McGuire, *Diary of a Southern Refugee*, p. 256.
17. Lee, Jr., *Recollections and Letters*, p. 159.
18. Freeman, *R. E. Lee*, vol. 4, p. 295.
19. Foote, *The Civil War*, vol. 2, p. 306.
20. Connelly, *The Marble Man*, p. 196.
21. Freeman, *R. E. Lee*, vol. 2, p. 131.

22. Dowdey, *Lee*, p. 583, contains the complete proclamation.

23. Freeman, *R. E. Lee*, vol. 4, p. 144.

24. Ibid., p. 147.

25. Dowdey, *Lee*, p. 322.

26. Lacey, *Majestic*, p. 35.

27. I Corinthians 14:8.

28. Freeman, vol. 1, p. 445.

29. Lee, Jr., *Recollections and Letters*, p. 120.

30. Freeman, *R. E. Lee*, vol. 3, p. 139, fn. 33.

31. Connelly, *The Marble Man*, p. 189.

32. Dowdey, *Lee*, p. 663.

33. Freeman, *R. E. Lee*, vol. 4, p. 295.

34. Flood, *Lee, the Last Years*, p. 206.

35. Freeman, *R. E. Lee*, vol. 4, p. 441.

36. Bowie, *The Master*.

37. Connelly, *The Marble Man*, p. 162.

BIBLIOGRAPHY

General References

Anonymous. *General Robert E. Lee*. Richmond, 1873.

Aurelias, Marcus. *Meditations*.

Bales, Richard. *The Confederacy*. (Music of the South during the years 1861–1865), Columbia Records.

Battles and Leaders of the Civil War. Vols. 2 and 4. New York: The Century Co., 1888 and 1956.

Beard, Charles, and Mary Beard. *The Rise of American Civilization*. 2 vols. New York, 1927.

Bill, Alfred Hoyt. *The Beleagured City*. New York, 1946.

Bradford, Gamaliel. *Lee, The American*. Boston: Houghton Mifflin, 1929.

Bond, Christiana. *Memories of General Robert E. Lee*. Baltimore: Normen Remington Co., 1926.

Brock, R. A., ed. *Gen. Robert Edward Lee*. Atlanta, 1897.

Brodie, Fawn M. *Thomas Jefferson*. New York, 1974.

Brownlaw, W. S. *Secession*. Philadelphia, 1862.

Bryan, J., III. *The Sword Over The Mantel*. New York: McGraw-Hill, 1960.

Catton, Bruce. *Glory Road*. Garden City, 1952.

———. *Mr. Lincoln's Army*. Garden City, 1954.

———. *A Stillness at Appomattox*. Garden City, 1954.

———. *This Hallowed Ground*. Garden City, 1956.

———. *The Coming Fury*. Garden City. 1961.

———. *Terrible Swift Sword*. Garden City, 1965.

———. *Never Call Retreat*. Garden City, 1965.

Chesnut, Mary Boykin. *A Diary from Dixie*. Edited by Ben Ames Williams. Cambridge, Massachusetts: Harvard University Press, 1980.

118

Christian, William Asbury. *Richmond, Her Past and Present*. Richmond, 1912.

Churchill, Winston S. *A History of the English Speaking Peoples*. Vol. 4. New York, 1958.

Commager, Henry Steele. *America's Robert E. Lee*. Boston, 1951.

Connelly, Thomas L. *The Marble Man*. New York: Alfred A. Knopf, 1977.

Craton, Michael. *A History of the Bahamas*. London: Collins, 1962.

Crenshaw, Ollinger. *General Lee's College*. New York, 1969.

Cooke, Allistair. *Six Men*. New York, 1977.

Cooke, John Esten. *Stonewall Jackson*. New York, 1886.

Cullins, Mary P. *The Lee Girls*. Winston-Salem, n.d.

Cummings, Kate. *The Journal of a Confederate Nurse*. Richard Barksdale Harwell, Editor. Baton Rouge, 1959.

Dabney, R. L. *Life and Campaigns of Lieutenant General Thomas J. Jackson*. New York, 1866.

Dabney, Virginius. *Richmond*. New York, 1977.

Davis, Burke. *To Appomattox*. New York City, 1981.

Davis, William C. *Battle at Bull Run*. Baton Rouge, 1977.

Douglas, Henry Kyd. *I Rode With Stonewall*. Chapel Hill: University of North Carolina Press, 1940.

Dowdey, Clifford. *Experiment in Rebellion*. Garden City, 1946.

———. *The Land They Fought For*. Garden City, 1955.

———. *Death of a Nation*. New York, 1958.

———. *Lee's Last Campaign*. Boston, 1960.

———. *Wartime Papers*, with Louis H. Manarin as co-editor. Boston, 1961.

———. *Lee*. Boston, 1965.

———. *The Seven Days*. Boston, 1985.

Earle, Peter. *Robert E. Lee*. London: Saturday Review Press, 1973.

Earle, Robert. *Pictoral Life of Robert E. Lee*.

Fairfax County, Virginia – A History. Fairfax, Virginia, 1978.

Fishwick, Marshall W. *Lee After The War*. New York: Dood, Mead and Co., 1963.

Fishwick, Marshall W. *Robert E. Lee: Churchman*. (Diocese of Southwestern Virginia Number 2). Living History Series.

Flood, Charles Bracelen. *Lee, The Last Years*. Boston: Houghton Mifflin, 1981.

Foote, Shelby. *The Civil War*. 3 Vols. New York, 1974.

Freeman, Douglas Southall. *R.E. Lee*. 4 vols. New York: Scribner's, 1934–35.

———. *Lee's Lieutenants*. 3 vols. New York: Scribner's, 1945–56.

————. *George Washington.* 6 vols. New York, 1948–54.

————. *Lee of Virginia.* New York, 1948.

Gerson, Noel B. *Light Horse Harry.* New York, 1966.

Glass, Paul, and Louis C. Singer. *Singing Soldiers.* New York, 1968.

Gordon, John B. *Reminiscences of the Civil War.* New York: Morningside Bookshop, 1981.

Grant, U. S. *Personal Memoirs.* Vol. 2. New York, 1886.

Henrick, Burton J. *The Lees of Virginia.* New York, 1926.

Hill, Merton E. *American Patriotism.* New York, 1926.

Hoehling, A. A., editor. *Vicksburg: 27 Days of Siege.* Englewood Cliffs, 1969.

Hood, J. B. *Advance and Retreat.* New Orleans, 1880.

Johnston, J. E. *Narrative of Military Operations.* New York, 1874.

Johnstone, William J. *Robert E. Lee, the Christian.* New York, 1933.

Jones, J. B. *A Rebel War Clerk's Diary.* 2 vols. Edited by Howard Swiggett. New York, 1935.

Jones, J. William. *Personal Reminiscences, Anecodotes, and Letters of General Robert E. Lee.* New York, 1874.

————. *Christ in the Camp.* Richmond: B. F. Johnson and Co., 1887.

————. *Life and Letters of Robert Edward Lee, Soldier and Man.* Washington, 1906.

Jones, Virgil Carrington. *Eight Hours Before Richmond.* New York, 1957.

Junior League. *The City of Washington.* New York, 1977.

Kane, Harnet T. *The Lady of Arlington.* Garden City, 1953.

Lee, Edmund Jennings. *Lee of Virginia: 1642–1892.* Philadelphia: Franklin Printing Co., 1895.

Lee, Fitzhugh, *General Lee,* New York, 1894.

Lee, Robert E. *To Markie.* Edited by Avery Crane. Cambridge, 1933.

Lee, R. E., Jr. *Recollections and Letters of General Robert E. Lee.* Garden City, 1904.

Long, A. L. *Memoirs of Robert E. Lee.* New York, 1886.

Long, E. B. *The Civil War Day by Day.* New York: Doubleday, 1971.

MacDonald, Rose M. E. *Mrs. Robert E. Lee.* Boston: Ginn and Co., 1939.

Marshall, John. *The Life of George Washington.* 5 vols. London: Walton Book Co., 1807.

Mason, Emily V. *Popular Life of General Robert Edward Lee.* Baltimore, 1872.

Maury, Dabney H. *Recollections of a Virginian.* New York, 1894.

McCabe, James D., Jr. *The Life and Campaigns of General Robert E. Lee.* Philadelphia, 1870.

McClellan, H. B. *The Campaigns of Stuart's Cavalry.* New York, 1885.

McGuire, Judith W. *Diary of a Southern Refugee During the War.* Richmond: University of Nebraska Press, 1995.

McPherson, James M. *Battle Cry of Freedom.* New York, 1988.

Meredith, Roy. *The Face of Robert E. Lee.* New York: Scribner's, 1947.

Mydral, Gunnary. *An American Dilemma.* New York, 1944.

Myers, Robert E., editor. *The Children of Pride.* London, 1972.

Nisbet, James Cooper. *Four Years on the Firing Line.* Edited by Bell Irvin Wiley. Jackson, Tennessee, 1963.

Parke, Joseph H. *General Leonidas Polk, C.S.A.* Baton Rouge, 1962.

Price, William H. *The Civil War Handbook.* Fairfax, Va.: L. B. Prince Co., 1961.

Roberts, Carey, and Rebecca Seely. *Tidewater Dynasty.* New York, 1982.

Sanborn, Margaret. *Robert E. Lee: A Portrait 1807–1861.* Philadelphia: Lippincott, 1966.

———. *Robert E. Lee: The Complete Man 1861–1870.* New York: J. B. Lippincott Co., 1967.

Sanburg, Carl. *Abraham Lincoln: The War Years.* 4 vols. New York: Harcourt, Brace and World, 1939.

Scott, Mary Wingfield. *Houses of Old Richmond.* Richmond, 1941.

———. *Old Richmond Neighbors.* Richmond, 1950.

Shaara, Michael. *The Killer Angels.* New York, 1974.

Smith, Page. *Trial by Fire.* New York, 1982.

Snow, William F. *Lee and His Generals.* New York, 1867.

Stern, Philip Van Doran. *Robert E. Lee: The Man and Soldier.* New York: McGraw-Hill, 1963.

Stewart, George R. *Pickett's Charge.* Cambridge, Massachusetts, 1959.

Strode, Hudson. *Jefferson Davis: Tragic Hero.* New York, 1959.

Taylor, Walter H. *Four Years With General Lee.* New York, 1877.

Trueblood, Elton. *Abraham Lincoln: Theologian of American Anguish.* New York: Harper and Row, 1973.

Tucker, Glenn. *High Tide at Gettysburg.* New York, 1958.

Vandiver, Frank E. *Mighty Stonewall.* New York, 1957.

Wharton, H. W. *War Songs and Poems of the Southern Confederacy.* Philadelphia, 1904.

Wheeler, Richard. *We Knew Stonewall Jackson*. New York, 1977.

Wiley, Bell Irvin. *The Common Solider in the Civil War*. Books 1 and 2. New York, 1943 and 1951.

Williams, T. Harry. *Lincoln and His Generals*. New York, 1952.

Winston, Robert W. *Robert E. Lee*. New York, 1934.

Young, Bennett H. *Confederate Wizards of the Saddle*. Kennesaw, Georgia, 1958.

Young, James C. *Marse Robert*. New York, 1929.

Religious and Other References

Addresses and Historical Papers, Diocese of Virginia, 1785–1885.

Augustine, St. *Confessions*. Whitney J. Oates, editor. New York, 1948.

Bayne, Stephen F., Jr. *Christian Living*. New York, 1957.

Bowie, Walter Russell. *The Master*. New York, 1958.

Brown, Lawrence L. *The Episcopal Church in Texas, 1838–1874*. Austin, 1963.

Browne, Edward Harold. *Exposition of the Thirty-nine Articles*. 1864, American Edition, 1874.

Brownell, Thomas Church. *The Family Prayer Book and Commentary*. New York, 1841.

Browning, E. B. *Sonnets from the Portuguese*. New York: Doubleday, 1954.

Bryden, George MacLaren. *Virginia's Mother Church*. 2 vols. Richmond, 1947.

Buechner, Frederick. *Wishful Thinking*. New York, 1973.

Burnett, White, editor. *The Spirit of Man*. New York, 1958.

Buttrick, George A. *Prayer*. New York, 1942.

Cather, Willa. *Death Comes for the Archbishop*. New York, 1951.

Cheshire, Joseph Blount. *The Church and the Confederate States*. New York, 1912.

Clebach, William, editor. *Journals of the Protestant Episcopal Church in the Confederate States of America*. Austin, 1962.

Coleridge, Samuel Taylor. *Notes on the Book of Common Prayer*. London, 1893.

Como, James T., editor. *C. S. Lewis at the Breakfast Table*. New York, 1979.

Daniel, Evan. *The Prayer Book*. London, 1913.

Eliot, T. S. *Selected Essays*. London: Harcourt, Brace and World, 1932.

———. *Complete Poems and Plays, 1909–1950*. New York, 1962.

Funk, Joseph. *Genuine Church Music*. Winchester, Virginia, 1835.

Gilkey, Langdon. *Message and Existence*. Seabury Press, 1979.

Goodwin, William A. R. *History of the Theological Seminary in Virginia*. 2 vols. Rochester, New York, 1923.

Hammarskjold, Dag. *Markings*. New York: Alfred A. Knopf, 1964.

Harkness, Georgia. *The Dark Night of the Soul*. New York, 1945.

Hawes, Francis L. *Contributions to the Ecclesiastical History of the U.S.A.* Vol. 1. New York, 1836.

Henshar, J. P. K. *Memoirs of the Life of the Rt. Rev. Richard Channing Moore, D.D.* Philadelphia, 1843.

Higgins, John. *This Means of Grace*. New York, 1945.

Hobart, J. H., editor. *The Christian's Manual*. New York, 1814.

Horton, F. P. *The Elements of the Spiritual Life*. London, 1960.

Inge, W. R. *Personal Religion and the Life of Devotion*. London: Longmans, Green and Co., 1924.

The Interpreter's Bible. 12 vols. Nashville, 1953.

Johns, John. *A Memoir of the Life of the Rt. Rev. William Meade, D.D.* Baltimore, 1869.

Kaufman, Gordon D. *The Theological Imagination*. Philadelphia, 1981.

Lacey, Robert. *Majestic: Elizabeth II and the House of Windsor*. Harcourt, Brace, and World, 1977.

Latourette, Kenneth Schott. *A History of Christianity*. New York, 1953.

Leaves of Gold: An Anthology. Brownlow, 1938.

Lewis, C. S. *Mere Christianity*. New York, 1943.

———. *The Four Loves*. New York, 1960.

———. *A Mind Awake – An Anthology*. Clyde S. Silby, editor. New York, 1969.

MacDonald, Margaret Simms. *White Already To Harvest*. Sewanee, 1975.

Manross, Wm. Wilson. *A History of the American Episcopal Church*. New York, 1959.

McConnell, S. B. *History of the American Episcopal Church*. New York, 1894.

McKim, Randolph A. *Washington's Church*. Germantown, 1877.

McLaughlin, William G., and Robert N. Bellah. *Religion in America*. Boston, 1968.

Meade, William. *Old Churches and Families of Virginia*. 2 vols. Philadelphia, 1861.

———. *Letters to a Mother*. Philadelphia, 1860.

Micklem, Nathaniel. *This Is Our Faith*. Printed in Great Britain.

Miller, Calvin. *The Singer*. Downers Grove, Illinois, 1975.

Minnegerode, Charles. *Sermons*. St. Paul's Church, Richmond, 1880.

Newton, Joseph Fort. *Live, Love and Learn*. New York, 1943.

Niebuhr, Reinhold. *The Nature and Destiny of Man*. 2 vols. New York: Scribner's, 1941.

Packard, Joseph. *Recollections of a Long Life: 1812–1902*. Washington, 1902.

Paton, Alan. *Instrument of Thy Peace*. New York, 1968.

Sayers, Dorothy L. *Creed or Chaos*. New York, 1949.

Sheen, Vincent. *Lead Kindly Light*. New York, 1949.

Shepherd, Massey H., Jr. *The Oxford American Prayer Book Commentary*. New York, 1950.

Smith, Hannah Whithall, editor. *Brother Lawrence*. New York, 1895.

Sockman, Ralph N. *The Higher Happiness*. Abingdon-Cokesbury Press, 1950.

Temple, William. *Christian Faith and Life*. London, 1931.

———. *The Hope of a New World*. New York, 1942.

———. *The Church Looks Forward*. New York, 1944.

———. *Readings of St. John's Gospel*. London, 1955.

Vache, C. Charles. *A History of Trinity Parish (Portsmouth)*. Portsmouth, Virginia, 1962.

Walker, Cornelius. *The Life of the Rev. William Sparrow*. Philadelphia, 1876.

Walker, Wiliston. *The History of the Christian Church*. New York, 1934.

Weddell, Elizabeth Wright. *St. Paul's Church (Richmond)*. 2 vols. Richmond, 1931.

Wilmer, Rich H. *Reminiscences*. New York, 1887.

Wood, John Sumner. *The Virginia Bishop*. Richmond, 1961.

Wright, Ronald Selby, editor. *Asking Them Questions*. 2 vols. Edinburgh, 1938, and London, 1950.

Holy Bible, King James' Version.

The *Book of Common Prayer*, 1789, 1928, and 1979.

The *Hymnal of the Episcopal Church*, 1940, 1982.

Monographs, Addresses, Articles, etc.

The Parish Register, Christ Church, Alexandria, Virginia.

The Parish Register, St. Paul's Church, Richmond, Virginia.

Catalogues of the Virginia Theological Seminary, 1850–1860.

Cheek, Mary Tyler Freeman. "Site of a Signal Victory." Historic Richmond Foundation, Spring 1980.

Cleaveland, George J. "The Thirty-nine Articles of Religion." (Unpublished).

——— Congressional Record, 94th Congress, First Session, 1975.

Coxe, R. Cleaveland. "Thoughts on Services." Baltimore, 1859.

Flyner, James T. "George Washington, Businessman." American Heritage, 1965.

Gaines, Francis F. "The Religion of Robert E. Lee." *Congressional Record*, Vol. 97, Part 2, 32nd Congress, First Session.

Jones, Everett H. "Bishop Steptoe Johnson." San Antonio, 1923.

Mollegan, A. T. "The Faith of Christians." Nine mimeographed lectures delivered in 1953.

———, *Southern Churchman*. Issues 1859 through 1869.

Sprunt, ——— W. "The Religious Faith of Robert E. Lee," Washington and Lee Magazine, Winter 1965.

"Stratford Hall," Robert E. Lee Foundation, 1935.